"I absolutely loved this book. I have read so many and can honestly say this is the one that really opened my eyes. It's fascinating and got me excited about the things I can achieve. It's a brilliant read. Anna has a very entertaining approach and light bulbs were exploding for me in every chapter. If you really want to get to grips with whatever is holding you back, this book will deliver."

Janette McNamara, Dublin, Ireland

"The enlightenment and joy I felt after reading the book is indescribable. I started drawing my Avatar and realised that Spielberg is nothing next to our true nature's authenticity. Look out world, I am releasing my best self!"

Roxana Cotruta, Athens, Greece

"Take the headset off! Anna takes us on a journey as we get to discover that we live life wearing a mask (really appropriate, considering the timing), whether it's the one we are looking through or the one we let others look through - REALITY is virtual! By enlightening us and allowing us to see the paradigm that is life, we awaken and discover we are able to implement sustainable tools and tactics to find our own music and game of life. Play On!"

Keith Cole, Johannesburg, South Africa

"This book has had a profound influence on me and how I want to face the reality of my life after reading this book. I know my life can be better from now."

Jindan Sun, Melbourne, Australia

"I read, stopped and thought - I had so many 'wow' moments reading this book. I wish it was written many years ago and someone had given it to me when I was fresh out of high school and starting university! How different my whole outlook on life and my mindset would have been. I've read the book a few times and certain parts I've read over and over because it's my own personal and constant reminder that I AM in control - the conscious me, here and now. I would highly recommend this book from high school students to, well, infinity and beyond!"

Sharon Mowat, Melbourne, Australia

"Self-sabotage is what I always do when something good is on the horizon. Understanding that this is not the way things need to be, with the help of the strategies in this book I can make changes for my highest good going forward. Thank you, Anna!"

Nicola Brettell-Smith, Winchester, England

"This book finally put in place the missing knowledge I needed to break out of my 'stuckedness' (yes, I made up this word). With brutal honesty Anna lays out the reasons behind, and the way through, my many failed attempts to change. With patience, understanding and great intuitive style, Anna has written a blueprint for consolidated change. It's not easy but at the same time simple in its elegance, so obvious when she shows how. A better, rewarding and fulfilling life awaits all who read."

Bret Chalmers, Melbourne, Australia

"Anna does a beautiful job of explaining the conscious and subconscious parts of ourselves and provides practical, actionable tools to wire your beliefs so that they support you unconditionally in your pursuit of a magnificent, consciously designed life."

Juliana Uto, Calgary, Canada

"Loved this book. The coding of our lives was a relatively new idea to me, and this book explains it in a way which is easy to understand and gives you the power to change your own coding through carefully and thoroughly guided techniques. A book you can go back to again and again!"

Karen Searle, Brisbane, Australia

"The author has an excellent understanding of the concepts necessary to shift your mind and realize a better life experience. She walks you through a step-by-step process of retraining your brain by reframing old beliefs into new possibilities to take you to a whole new level of living."

Joanne Mengwasser, St Louis, USA

"A great concept explained in clear, understandable words. Going through the book, I have noticed patterns in reviewing my life, my actions, thoughts and feelings and the often windy paths they have led me to. Thanks to the brilliant questions and the workbook, I am now able to course-correct and create new coding for a much more exciting and inspiring future. Thank you, Anna, for your expert support to 'Escape the Matrix' which is no longer serving us."

Claudia Duncan, Ratzeburg, Germany

Quantum Mind Academy

ESCAPE YOUR *MATRIX*
How to Master The Game Of Life

Copyright: Quantum Mind Academy, 2020

First Published 2020
Published by Quantum Mind Academy

Email: anna@quantummindacademy.com
Website: www.quantummindacademy.com

All rights reserved. Without limiting the rights under copyright reserved above, no part of this publication may be reproduced, stored in or introduced in a database and retrieval system or transmitted in any form or any means without prior written permission of the author.

ISBN: 978-0-6450159-3-5

Special thanks to Tracey Bigg for all her support in editing this book and making it a reality! Couldn't have done it without you, Tracey!!

ESCAPE YOUR
MATRIX

How To Master The Game Of Life

Anna Berger
www.quantummindacademy.com

PLEASE NOTE:

This book comes with a private, downloadable journal which will guide you through self-analysis. This journal is a digital workbook where you can record your thoughts and make notations – or you can print it if you wish – rather than writing in this book.

You can find it on our website at www.quantummindacademy.com under the section: BOOK.
To access, please enter the password: **CODING101**

Go ahead and get it before you start reading.

Here is YOUR MISSION, SHOULD YOU CHOOSE TO ACCEPT IT

I dare you to take this 45-day challenge of designing your blueprint and re-coding your subconscious mind to follow your Life's Purpose.

15 days to read this book and finish your journal, and
30 days of re-coding!

I can't wait to hear what results and synchronicities you will encounter.

Send me an email at anna@quantummindacademy.com or comment on our Facebook page to let me know what transformations you have been able to achieve! I look forward to hearing from you!

CONTENTS

1. WELCOME TO 'THE MATRIX' 7
Arrival And Programing.. 9
Simply Confirmed – Why Are You Always Right?........... 18
Your Internal Voice – Customized Siri............................... 27
YOUR Mind – The Master Manipulator............................. 29
The Masks We Wear.. 38
Stuck On You – Attachment Theory................................... 52

2. AWAKENING.. 67
Fooled By The Biggest Illusion... 78
How To Master The Game Of Life.................................... 89
Catch The Thief On Time... 91

3. PREPARATION FOR THE GREAT ESCAPE..................... 97
Find Your Groove... 100
Create A Blueprint – The Game Changer....................... 113
Create Your Avatar.. 138

4. ESCAPING YOUR MATRIX – A.K.A MISSION POSSIBLE.. 147
Can't Get You Out Of My Mind.. 149
Coding 101 For 'Dummies'.. 160

5. LIFE BEYOND 'THE MATRIX'.. 169
Follow The 'White Rabbit'... 171
Flashlight Theory... 176

7 Wisdoms To Live By 178
With A Little Help From My Friends 181

Glossary 187
Sources of Inspiration and Wisdom 191
About the Author: 197

FOREWORD
By Karlin Sloan
CEO, Sloan Group International

Dear Reader,

Anna Berger is the coach you always wanted – someone who has been there at the cutting edge of business and entrepreneurship as a strategic leader, someone who's awakened to their own resilience and strength of character, someone who sees possibility in every scenario, and someone who cares deeply about helping you to become what you're capable of becoming.

Anna can transform a company, and, more importantly, she will transform your life.

Anna has committed herself to finding the best thinkers in whatever discipline she's passionate about and learning from masters, then becoming a master herself. She is a true Renaissance Woman!

When I met Anna she had just come back from a photo shoot. When Anna got interested in photography she didn't mess around! She went to the top photographers in the world and learned directly from them, then created her own incredible artwork all around the globe for the joy of that creation.

From Oprah to Tony Robbins to Bruce Lipton, Anna connects to thinkers who change the world and make things happen, integrates their thinking with her own and synthesizes it into practical, actionable tools for those she works with.

Now is such a potent time for breaking through our mental programming to create a healthier, more sustainable, more joyful, just and peaceful world.

With much of the globe reeling from economic and health related crises, many of us are stepping back and assessing who we are, what we really care about, and who we wish to become. As poet Mary Oliver asks… 'What will you do with your one wild and precious life?'

Now is your time.

Anna has created a powerful system that enables us to do a deep dive into the masks we wear and the perspectives we've adopted over a lifetime, allowing us to wake up and break through to our own greatness and FREEDOM OF MIND to fill our lives with passion and purpose.

I invite you to take the journey that lies ahead in this book, and to really grab hold of the exercises and journaling available to you in this program. It will be just what you were looking for, and nothing like you expected.

Enjoy!

Karlin Sloan
CEO, Sloan Group International
Author of the Amazon #1 bestseller Inspiring Leadership for Uncertain Times, Smarter, Faster, Better, and Lemonade: The Leaders Guide to Resilience at Work

Introduction

Have you ever felt like your mind is equivalent to having 27 tabs open on your computer, eight of them not loading properly, stuck in the circle, and you have no idea where the heck the music is coming from? Welcome to the average person's mind! Unfortunately, for all of us overachievers who constantly seek self-improvement, the way we deal with those issues is through positive thinking, huge to-do lists, New Year's resolutions, super-strong will, shortcuts and hacks...more learning, more '10 steps to this' and '10 steps to that'...and the list goes on.

I have been a business and a life coach for over a decade and have been teaching all my overachieving clients the tricks, shortcuts and life hacks to success. It's the business coach version of a badass trainer in the gym.

Psychology, philosophy, human potential, success coaching, NLP, hypnosis and quantum physics have always interested me. In my early 20s I was lucky enough to get involved in a few awesome self-development training programs, and read hundreds of books that set me on a path of never-ending learning, building a very successful business through hard work and a mindset of *'anything is possible'*, and after exiting the business I was living life to the max, a.k.a. ticking off the most amazing bucket list. I was also helping others build big businesses and a happy life.

During my years as a coach I found that a lot of businesses eventually came to a glass ceiling and couldn't grow larger due to the owner's path in life and the business's path not being aligned. Therefore, my business coaching would often shift to life coaching, working out the reason why a business was started in the first place, and working out what a business owner **really** wanted out of their life. Once the personal and business paths were aligned, the ceiling got removed and the business went 'through the roof'!

With all those 'hacks' and shortcuts I have been teaching my clients for years, I really thought I was on top of my game. After all, my clients were getting what I thought were outstanding results...until I came across this.

It wasn't until I got thrown off a Friesian horse, straight underneath the hooves at full gallop, and had a near-death experience that I was forced to slow down. Some of my injuries that made my life go from a million miles per hour to a snail's pace recovery finally gave me some 'me time' to stumble across something quite remarkable.

I threw myself into a quest of discovery. As a believer of things happening for a reason, I figured there might be more to the story than a silly horse-riding accident. Some might believe that it was the 'Universe' telling me to slow down; who knows, maybe it was. I, however, had a hunch that it was my subconscious mind playing tricks on me again...

While trying to recover, with limited movement and plenty of time, I dove into the soul-searching 'Why am I here?' enquiry. And the secret that I have discovered was so mind-blowing that it literally catapulted me into a state of such bliss and calmness like I have never experienced before. And, no, it wasn't the painkilling drugs I was taking. The calmness, clarity and obviousness were so astonishing that, at first, they made me laugh out loud. I saw the world in a new light. I saw all the

stresses, anxieties, depressions, heartbreaks and problems I have ever experienced disappear in a split second.
But what's even more exciting is that this discovery is so profound that I have no doubt in believing that, once shared, it can literally change the world as we know it...for much, much, much better!!

See, what I have discovered is that there is a 'shut-down/reset button'! A factory setting that out of confusion and stresses will bring you back to the magnificent human being you were meant to be in the first place, in the blink of an eye!

It came to me through an 'aha moment' of simply just getting it...it's like finally realizing that the world is round and not flat. It put **everything** into a whole new perspective!

Stay with me, I'll try to explain this paradigm shift to you in the simplest possible form. This stuff isn't new. These are some of the teachings of various enlightened people of the past: the Socrates, Edisons and Einsteins of this world. They have also been taught to us by some spiritual leaders but so often either misunderstood by many or avoided due to stigmas (i.e. different religions) attached.

The concepts have been disclosed in many forms but are either dressed up in super-scientific jargon of quantum physics or experienced by yogis, who to a lot of humans are just those bold dudes sitting on the mountains of Nepal with clearly nothing better to do.

For years I considered myself a very driven, goal-oriented intellectual – a businessperson – and the idea of exposing myself to a 'spiritual world' was just too airy-fairy for me. I got only as far as watching 'The Secret', which I used often to tick off my bucket list items, like hanging out with Oprah, traveling the world and doing fun stuff. This is another pretty cool tool to have in your arsenal of tricks. Little did I know that this was just the entry level to the exciting world of incredible adventure!

This book will walk you step by step through your own journey. I am hoping it will become the sunbeam that will illuminate your world, put a spotlight on your own shadows and help you create the most exciting path forward...

This book is divided into five parts:

1. **Welcome to 'The Matrix'** – will show you how your subconscious mind has been manipulated from day one, and by the age of seven your 'operating system' of your own mind has been dangerously set for life. This section will walk you through certain filters which have determined who you are right now and why any stretch beyond this point (regardless of how hard you work) can easily be derailed by self-sabotage. Once you understand it, everything will become remarkably clear.

This section will also show you how your current conditioning has affected all your past and present intimate relationships in your life – an absolute enlightenment for some!

2. **Awakening** – will walk you through a huge paradigm shift to see your life in a different 'dimension' – mind-blowing!

3. **Preparation for the Great Escape** – will give you three brilliant tools to redefine your ultimate dream life:

a. <u>Find Your Groove</u> – will help you define what is your real purpose in life.
   b. <u>Create a Blueprint</u> – will show you how to put your whole life under a proverbial microscope and analyze 12 categories, from your health, love life and career to friendships, adventures and everything in between. You will learn how to create a custom-made, personalized blueprint, or map, that will get you from where you are today to a life beyond your wildest dreams.
   c. <u>Create Your Avatar</u> – will show you how to improve your own character to be able to achieve all the goals you set in your blueprint.

4. **Escaping Your Matrix – A.K.A Mission <u>Possible</u>** – will show you how to re-code your own subconscious mind – FREE, 100% DIY and no computer skills required!

5. **Life Beyond 'The Matrix'** – will open your eyes and heart to what's possible in the life beyond 'The Matrix'.

Welcome to your own journey of escaping 'Your Matrix'.

PART 1
Welcome to 'The Matrix'

What exactly is 'The Matrix' that I am referring to? Some of you might have come across the word 'matrix' in mathematics, in biology or just in a brilliant blockbuster movie you once watched called 'The Matrix'. To avoid any confusion, in this book my reference to 'The Matrix' is the conditioning of your mind or a restrictive program it is currently stuck in. It is the limit of your current thinking. I know this might sound a little weird right now but, as you explore the concepts in this book, it will become super, super clear. All you have to do is keep an open mind and read on.

Arrival And Programing

Just contemplate this for a minute: what if you were a spiritual being who was lucky enough to experience life in a human form, coming from, let's call it, a 'Spirit Planet' to Planet Earth for a little while...and what if some of your 'buddies' were less lucky; they came back as a fly, a tree, a rabbit, a corn – only you, as a human, had the ability to be conscious...

Back on your 'Spirit Planet' you won the lucky prize to go back into 'the game' as a human. In mathematical terms, the chance of your being born to the exact parents and making it through the sperm selection is approximately 14 trillion to one – congratulations, you made it through!

Oh, the joy of new experiences!

So, you rock up in someone's uterus and grow your limbs and body's organs until you are ready to face the world. Nine months later you arrive into the world with a slap on your butt. You scream! This warm fuzzy feeling of love and security you had while back on the 'Spirit Planet', where everybody is connected, is over – you are out on your own, greeted by some doctor in a mask and other humans who are either happy or unhappy that you have arrived. The game starts.

Within a day you are given a name, a family, a culture, a religion and a whole bunch of new rules you need to learn and follow. You also learn that on this planet everything seems separate. You are you, mother is someone else, father is the one with a beard, here is a dog and a flower, a cat and a tree. You don't even realize they are all energy spirits thrown into different forms – all on their own – with survival mechanisms built into their game mode...in humans, called the mind.

When you arrive as a brand new baby, at first you trust everything in your midst, assuming that everyone around you is as pleasant, connected and ever-loving as on 'Spirit Planet'. It takes you a little while to discover that you now have senses connected - you can see, you can smell, you can touch and taste and also hear. Awesome!

You first arrived on Planet Earth with no knowledge – you arrived like a cute little empty container. Happy, smiley and oblivious to the world, the only way you can figure out how to behave is by the reflection of people around you. Are they smiling back at me? Am I safe? Do they love me?

After all, you were all about love and belonging when you first arrived, so you were assuming that you would be taken care of and loved. But soon enough you learned that love is not all there is. Sometimes they would smile, sometimes they would frown. Sometimes they would sing, sometimes they would yell. You were hypersensitive to the sounds, sights and energy around you. By observing the world around you, you learned quickly that love on Planet Earth is conditional.

Love was given as long as you followed the **rules** – rules that made you fit into your new tribe. You were allowed to do this; you were not allowed to do that. This is how you should act, this is what is polite to say, this is how you behave...you get the picture!

You went through your childhood learning new skills like walking and talking, and being constantly conditioned by those around you. Mostly with great intentions, you were being taught how to become a great human being and become self-sufficient. Your sense of belonging and love never made you question the status quo – the world around you was perfect (even if it wasn't, you assumed it was) and your job was to learn how to **fit in**.

Your mind's job was to collect as much information in this container as quickly as possible so you could survive on your own.

All the information you received you stored in your memory. Your mind's job was to sort all that information into different files so that you were able to retrieve them easily. With every object or situation you ever came across, your memory would fetch a bunch of supporting documents (presented as thoughts/feelings) and your mind knew straight away what meaning to attach to it.

Let's say you see ice cream. Your mind fetches information from your memory bank: it's cold, it's sweet, grandma gives it to you, she loves it when you giggle, associated with love, associated with smiles, associated with positive feelings, associated with family time – within seconds your mind translates it into 'yum!'

Let's say you see a big dog. Your mind finds everything stored on that topic: barking, noise, scary, falling over, bigger than me, story somebody read about a big, bad wolf – translation of the mind: 'warning, be afraid!'

Your memory will retrieve a bunch of information which will be turned into meaning by your subconscious mind in a split second...so you don't get eaten up. Or burned by a hot iron. Or drowned...its job is to keep you away from pain and survive. And, if there is no threat, it will guide you towards pleasure.

Since we humans are quite a complicated species, it takes us a little longer to stop relying on our caretakers. It's the job of our tribe – parents, friends, grandmas, aunties with mustaches – to fill you in on all the information **they** know so you can become a great human being...just like them!

The subconscious mind acts like a self-learning computer program – except this one is EXTREMELY, EXTREMELY powerful. It learns through 'belief input' transmitted by others. In the early stages of life, all you do is take the information in and constantly code and code and code. Everything is being registered by your mind. Not only beliefs were transmitted but also experiences you went through and everything you observed. Every smile, every frown, every positive or negative bit of feedback from others was recorded in your memory. Your mind was diligently coding your personalized map, which would become a blueprint for the rest of your life.

In fact, 80% of your knowledge that is currently stored in your subconscious mind was put there in the first seven years of your life! The rest was picked up from others via different experiences, including from teachers, books, school bullies, social media, bosses and Netflix. Whoopee!

By the way, the stuff you just picked up from others after the age of seven...guess where 80% of that came from? Yep, those people's aunties with mustaches!

Up to roughly the age of seven your brain works on only theta vibration waves (same as in hypnosis), meaning you have absolutely **no ability** to reason as to what comes in – you just accept everything as given. The cute little container, collecting information. Writing a program, which will become your blueprint – a recording to be played over and over again for the rest of your life. The dangerous code that will determine the quality of your life until you die...or until you wake up to it – whichever comes first!

So, whatever beliefs your tribe had at the time, they became **your** beliefs. Life is hard. Money doesn't grow on trees. I sacrifice myself for you. Other people's opinion of me is important. Dad is always right. Need to win that medal. Can't go out looking like that. We are not made of money. I get hurt if I share my true self. Men don't cry. Parents are always right. There is nothing to cry about. People are out there to get you. Don't trust strangers. Men are users. Respect the elderly. Be good. Make me proud. Don't question authority. Either do it properly or don't do it at all. Kids are to be seen but not heard. Toughen up. Wow! How many of these did you have installed in **your** mind?

By the way, these beliefs did not have to be statements somebody made. You were very, very observant. Attuned to the energy around you, you picked up on all the nuances. Your brother is mean, your grandma likes you, your grandpa ignores you, your mum has no time for you, your father thinks you are weak – whatever it was for you, you added it to your brilliant collection of beliefs.

Your mind is a constant meaning-making machine. It doesn't just record your experiences; it also gives them a meaning. All it took was for somebody to play a joke on you to create a meaning and a belief that people cannot be trusted. Another child to laugh at you to experience shame. A parent yelling or ignoring you to feel judged or abandoned. Not being invited to a party to feel like an outcast. A parent being too busy for you to code: unlovable. And the list goes on...

What's even more interesting is that not only were you coding those beliefs; you accepted that everything around you was perfection, even if it was totally screwed up. You didn't know any different, hence you assumed it was how it **should** be!

Grew up with a drunk parent? That's normal! Grew up in a broken home? That's normal. Grew up in a loving home? That's normal. Grew up abused? That's normal! Grew up with a helicopter parent? That's normal. Whatever environment you grew up in, especially in the first seven years of your life, while you were recording and coding your mind, you accepted that **everything** around you was **perfection**! And since at that age all children are egocentric – the whole world revolves around them – the only conclusion to come from that is the only thing that wasn't perfect was 'you'.

During those years, where all we wanted was to be fed, protected and loved, we looked up to our tribe for validation. And every time we got negative feedback we automatically assumed that we were not good enough. The tougher the childhood, the bigger the 'not enough-ness' we had established.

What do you think the chances are that while coding you had found examples that you were not strong enough, not brave enough, not lovable enough, not pretty enough, not smart enough and not (insert your own insecurity here)? Well, you know where I am going with this – extremely high!

It didn't help that our parents, as parents did before them, often taught us using negative reinforcement – you know, like a sports coach might do. Ever had a parent that wanted to 'toughen you up'? Or a teacher perhaps? This is so common, it isn't funny!

The 'tough love' approach is great when you are an adult and can reason for yourself. Say you are on a basketball team and your coach tells you, 'You are not good enough for the team.' As an adult you know the **meaning** of the words and translate them as 'I'd better get off my butt and train harder so that I won't let my teammates down'. Fantastic – you got the message! But just imagine if you were told this before you turned seven, when you are in theta level brain vibration and all you do is code. If you were told at an age when you have absolutely no ability to translate the meaning of words that 'you are not good enough for the team', you took it as gospel. Especially if those words were used in a situation where you experienced shame in front of others, not only was it devastating for you; it just made you inherit your new, forever-crippling insecurity: 'you are not enough' – congratulations!

It's only when you develop reasoning (usually after the age of seven, when our brain waves go up to the next level of this game – the alpha and beta vibrations) that you start seeing that sometimes parents, teachers or aunties with mustaches have something else on their mind and the words they use might have a slightly different meaning, for example words of encouragement through negative words, fondly referred to as reverse psychology!

Don't get me wrong, even when you are older your subconscious mind can still be screwed up by others. All it takes is a bully, a tragic incident or a serious heartbreak and your mind will ensure that you will avoid those scenarios for the rest of your life!

In fact, the 'Not Enough-ness' and 'Not Lovable' have become the biggest diseases of human existence. Every problem, stress, anxiety and depression can be linked to those two anchors deeply encoded in our minds.

Simply Confirmed – Why Are You Always Right?

But wait, there is more! If you thought engraving words 'you are not good enough' into your memory as a child was bad enough, wait till you hear about this other quirky program that kicks in – **the confirmation bias**.

The confirmation bias is, simply put, your subconscious mind's search for confirmation of your newly acquired belief and rejection of anything that is different from that belief.

There are **hundreds** of different biases (i.e. mind shortcuts) your mind indulges in, but confirmation bias is one that 'takes the cake'. There is so much information around us (sights, smells, sounds, etc.). In fact, there are over two million inputs of information per any given second, hence our mind, however powerful, cannot cope with the influx – it needs to filter through **relevant and useful** information only. Studies have shown that we can take in approximately only seven chunks of information at any given second (Mandrel and Shebo 1982) – the rest gets discarded as irrelevant.

What an object is and what it means to you are two totally different things. We will talk more about this in the upcoming chapter 'Awakening', but what's important for you to understand right now is that, with so much information flying your way, your mind has to make some kind of order out of that chaos and noise, and hence it will distort, reject and delete **most** of that information **unless** it confirms something that has already been coded in your beliefs.

Let me say this again: your mind is taking in only information which **confirms** your already established beliefs and **discards** anything that opposes it.

Every piece of information has to be funneled through numerous filters and compared to how they fit within your current beliefs, your values, your memories and your current attitude toward a subject. By the time they get into your mind most of the information out there gets discarded as irrelevant. Only seven chunks of info per second will make it through – and they are so distorted and personalized to your own experience that ALL they do is **support** your belief. Whatever dumbass belief you have adopted as a child, your mind will keep collecting more and more supportive data to confirm it – so that you are well-equipped to face the world!

Your subconscious mind does not have the ability to decide whether the information that you originally acquired is positive or negative, it does not know if it will have a positive impact on your life. It's not there to judge (in fact, there is no-one in there to do that anyway; it's just a program), hence your mind goes ahead and writes down: 'I am bad at…(insert your insecurity).' Remember, your mind's computer was designed to collect information to be a reference in the future in decision making. It's there to 'keep you safe' so you can live a long life. It also wants you to keep away from pain. If something caused pain originally, it will get coded as a WARNING sign to avoid in the future. It will NEVER ask you to question whether your first assumption or belief was correct!

If someone tells you as a child that you suck at singing, your subconscious mind will write it in the program and (since it wants to keep you away from pain, i.e. future embarrassment) through confirmation bias it will find lots and lots of examples that 'prove you right'. If you installed that belief at the age of five, by the time you get to adulthood and are placed in front of an audience behind a microphone, you'd 'rather die' than speak or sing. The number of files you have acquired on why you suck will be so overwhelming it will absolutely make you freeze!

For every 'truth' that you will accept into memory, you will find only supportive 'truths' out there which will strengthen your point of view. Your mind will become obsessed with collecting data on that topic. And it doesn't just collect – oh, no, it compounds it as well. It will make your 'argument' so strong that it will soon become part of your identity!

Your beliefs not only refer to yourself; they also refer to other people. Have you ever noticed how you make up your mind about somebody in a few seconds? You don't really know the person, but just one look at them and your mind takes a shortcut to a 'general group' it has created. Isn't it amazing how we all have opinions about celebrities based on a snippet of information we received from the media, even though we don't actually know the person?

I don't know about you but my subconscious mind has a whole library on the Kardashians and where in the world they fit – yet, funnily enough, I have never watched an episode of 'Keeping up with the Kardashians' and chances are if I were to trip over them I wouldn't even recognize them. Yet my mind has a full category for them and files upon files to prove me right. Interesting!

If your first impression of someone is that they are caring and loving, you will see only loving things about them. If you decide someone is mean, you will see only those things which will support your point of view. Look around you and ask yourself how you formed judgment about all the people you know...

Those early-formed beliefs will forever dictate the paths you will take in your adult life. Let's look at relationships...when you were growing up, if you observed an unhealthy relationship between your parents – guess what? That's **your** blueprint for future relationships! If you decided some time along the way that all men are users, or all women are after money – guess what?

Your mind will only prove you right – every single time! The longer you hold that belief, the more data your mind will collect to prove you are right – even if you were completely wrong to start with! This is a **massive** glitch in the program!

The lurking feeling of 'not being good enough' has been even more sped up now with access to the internet and the beautiful world of social media. We now don't compare ourselves to just our tribe, our schoolmates and our friends. Oh, no, now we can compare ourselves to millions of people around the world! Our confirmation bias is in 'ecstasy' – it can find so many examples of why our belief was right!

With our younger generations being drip-fed through social media, no wonder our suicide rate is going through the roof! No-one is questioning the status quo – where the original belief comes from or how ridiculously it was established. All we are obsessed about is how we prove the belief right!

Every time you shy away from doing something, realize that you are just hitting a block which was created in your childhood. It metaphorically acts like a handbrake thrown in while you are happily driving through life.

'Let's dance' – 'Ahhh, no, don't want to look stupid.'
'Let's sing' – 'Ummm, no, can't hold a tune to save my life.'
'Let's paint' – 'No, I'm really terrible at it.'
'Can you say a few words?' – 'Oh my goodness, I'm going to die from embarrassment.'

Ever come across any of these? That's just your handbrake kicking in! And, if you were to dig a little further, you'll probably find it got engraved onto your system before you turned seven.

The confirmation bias also gets very tragic in adult lives when adults start to form relationships. If a person's belief is that they are not lovable, it doesn't matter how wonderful a partner they will attract into their life – the chances are they will stuff up the relationship because they will constantly question 'Why would that person love me?' They will not believe it because their original conditioning made them believe that they are 'not lovable'. Hence, it won't make sense to them that somebody actually would love them. They will come up with sophisticated reasons why their partner is 'not for real'. Beliefs such as 'they are probably after my money', 'they just need someone to look after them' or 'they are just playing with me' are common. Everything is being seen through the lens of suspicion and any minor incidents are 'proof' that they were 'right' in the first place. What they will then do is push that person away because they cannot accept love for themselves; when somebody else says it, they can't believe it to be true. This is why they will **always** be seeking love and never find it.

They might desperately want love but **all** they will keep finding is reasons why someone wants to take advantage of them and is not for real. This is confirmation bias at its 'best' – very, very tragic! We will talk more about relationships shortly.

Ponder a little on any of those beliefs that you acquired as a child. I bet you'll find quite a few lurking in those memory compartments! A lot of them are so well hidden that you don't even know you have them. Confirmation bias is something you never really think about (even if you know it exists). All you know is what you know.

The trick is to always question your own status quo. If you want to become successful in life, think of yourself as a high-rise building: the bigger the building you would like to build, the bigger and stronger the foundations you need to have. If you don't clear the basement of limiting beliefs, of your lurking 'not enough-ness' (in whatever form you had coded them), the foundations will not be strong enough and will not sustain massive growth. Eventually they will take you down – in business, in relationships or in your own sanity…

Here is an example of one I found in my personal life – in a very painful way. It relates to the fact that the subconscious mind cannot deal with opposing beliefs. It will weigh them up and work out which is more important to you.

Before I got into coaching I had a very successful multimillion-dollar construction business, which I worked very hard to build from scratch. One day I attracted a business partner who, let's say it politely, 'took it all off me'. It's a long story that ended up in the Supreme Court, but the bottom line comes down to: why did I attract such a person into my business in the first place? After much deliberation, I realized that I had this belief in my subconscious mind that 'you cannot be wealthy and have true friends'. I believed that people only wanted to be friends with me because of my money and what I could do for them, and that I wasn't worthy of true friendships. And, since I valued friendships more than money, unconsciously I struggled with being wealthy. My subconscious mind couldn't deal with opposing beliefs, so it 'solved that problem' for me! It attracted somebody into my business who cheated me out of millions. Problem solved! Or so my mind thought.

How is that for a limiting belief?

It doesn't matter how successful you become in your life – if you have a hidden limiting belief, it will eventually take you down like a crushing torpedo!

And here is the kicker! The more intelligent you are, the more sophisticated examples you have created to justify your beliefs. Hopefully all the beliefs you have accumulated so far serve you well, but, if I were to take a guess, most people have those hidden 'handbrakes' buried deep down – so, the sooner we get them discovered, analyzed and decoded, the quicker you can reach your full potential!

In our later chapters we will explore all aspects of your life and see if we can find and replace some of the negative beliefs you have accumulated. For now, just be aware of them. If there comes a time when you feel uncomfortable doing something, ask yourself: 'Where did I learn to be afraid of this?'

Your Internal Voice – Customized Siri

As your subconscious mind collects all the information and stores it in your memory, your conscious mind tries to make sense of it by giving it a meaning. It does this with the help of a little friend – your internal voice. That little friend is sometimes also referred to as an inside voice or a thought chatter.

That friend can get a little annoying sometimes as it constantly talks…yap, yap, yap…and is the one who tells us 'it's OK to eat that ice cream, you can always diet tomorrow'.

And if you don't have one of those…it's the one that just asked you, 'What friend?'

What is the role of your inside voice? The voice in your head is nothing more than your mind's best buddy – its interpreter. Since your subconscious mind has been installed for your survival and to store a massive amount of data in your memory files, your inside voice is nothing more than your own customized 'Siri' (like the voice you have on mobile devices).

Siri constantly gathers information processed by your mind and delivers meaning to everything you are looking at. Just imagine a super-sophisticated version of a Siri (interpreter) sitting in your head. Not only does it retrieve the information for you, analyze things and make suggestions, but with some of us it often argues, criticizes and yells at us! That smart-ass little Siri!

You look at a sunset, your internal voice fetches a whole bunch of past experiences associated with the sunset (from the memory bank in your subconscious mind). It then throws it at you in the form of thoughts and feelings, and your 'Siri' translates its meaning to you.

Everything that you are currently experiencing is automatically viewed through your past experiences with your customized 'Siri' narrating it.

This is why you can have two people looking at the same sunset and one will be marveling at its beauty, while the other will shrug and say they've seen better.

YOUR Mind – The Master Manipulator

Since the subconscious mind has been installed in our being as a protection or guiding program, it has also self-learned how to become self-important. Since on Planet Earth we have divided ourselves into different entities (i.e. different bodies), without any instructions as to why we are here, we automatically assume that the aim of this game (living) is to become more important than others. After all, if we are more important, we will have a better chance of survival and being loved – or so our mind assumes.

We crave attention, love and admiration from those around us. We associate these needs with basic survival. Tony Robbins talks about **significance** as being one of the most powerful human needs, with 80% of the world having it as their **primary** need. Now, when you think about it, that totally sucks because it means that most of us will spend all our lives comparing ourselves to others and constantly competing for attention and importance.

Our subconscious mind has therefore developed interesting 'manipulations' which temporarily give us the energy and security we feel we need, the significance we crave. Like with everything else, we use these manipulations unconsciously.

These manipulations have been beautifully explained in one of my favorite books 'The Celestine Prophecy', via a reference to 'control dramas' and how we seek control of others due to our own fears and insecurities.

Ever felt emotionally drained after having a conversation with somebody? Ever met someone who constantly gets sick? Ever met those who get hot under the collar over random things? Have you ever had a friend who constantly criticizes? Ever met someone who is super-adventurous and mysterious? Yep, that's a manipulation in its full glory.

Here are four of the most known manipulations we develop. It is probably easier to pinpoint them in someone else, but, be assured, everybody is using them – your mind is also 'guilty as charged'! ☺

See if you can find which one your mind is using:

MANIPULATIONS

The 'Poor Me' Manipulation

This is the most passive of all the 'manipulations'. People who use it make you feel sorry for them. This traps you into connecting or reconnecting with them in sympathy, which shifts the energy and will control you.

Have you ever come across parents who are always busy and the only way they will stop and pay attention to their child is if the child gets hurt in some way? Yep...they have just engraved in their child's mind that the only way to get love from a parent is by doing something that will make them go, 'Oh, you poor thing, let me stop and give you a cuddle.' That kind of belief will soon turn into a manipulation played by the child – often not intentionally. The mind will, by using the confirmation bias, constantly get that person into situations where people around them will have to stop and say, 'Oh, you poor thing, let me stop and give you attention.'

With adults, their 'poor me' manipulation will also extend to make you feel like you did something wrong and were not 'there' for them in a time of need. They can also try to take you on a guilt trip by saying things like, 'After all I have done for you, you've let me down like this.'

This psychological manipulation suddenly throws you off balance and brings your attention and connection back to them, as you work out whether what they are saying is true. When the 'manipulation' fully works, you connect deeply with them, trying to make amends.

When this happens they feel good, but you, on the other hand, feel drained or weakened, being consumed by guilt. This is because they have seized control of the relationship the two of you have created, moving you into a kind of voluntary deferral to their dominance and self-importance. The significance shifts to them.

It's easy to spot whether this is a manipulation because, even if you think they might have a point and you try to comfort them, they never quite interact genuinely. They always carry the air of being wronged and make you feel guilty. No matter how attentive you are, they want more, and they often repeat their manipulation by throwing some other guilt-inducing accusation at you.

Most people do not realize that these manipulations are played out unconsciously – most of the time. You might have a highly intelligent person who constantly gets sick when they are stressed out. Or gets their ankle twisted or suffers from migraines. It's not that they get sick because, well, it's that time of year when people tend to catch cold – no, they get sick because their **powerful** computer program helps them deal with stress by attracting a situation which will help them with 'control'. Their mind is desperate for attention and control as if its survival depends on it. Understand that they are **not** pretending – their mind is literally controlling their biology and the 37.2 trillion cells it has at its command…

Quick fix

The solution is simple. Dr Eric Bern, in his brilliant book 'The Games People Play', advised a simple fix to help people break out of their manipulation: you 'name the game'. By naming the game you bring the interaction back to authenticity by honestly revealing how you feel.

This, by the way, is exactly what you have to do to stop any of the other manipulations as well.

One person cannot control you successfully unless you play along, to some extent.

Plainly say something such as, 'Sometimes I feel you try to make me feel guilty in order to control me.' What you are saying is the truth as you know it, and the truth always sets you, and the other person, free.

If for any reason they argue with you, or guilt trip you a little more, stick to your guns. Say, 'I am just telling you how I feel.' Pose it in that way because it is possible you are wrong about their intentions. If you're not, soon enough they will think twice before trying to manipulate you again.

The Aloof Manipulation

The Aloof manipulation baits you into connection by acting distant and unreadable. An Aloof person wants you to connect with them but they only partially connect themselves, while withholding information.

This manipulation is often developed in childhood as the 'rebel' – with either a 'helicopter' or overly critical parent.

An Aloof person leads you into the pursuit of more knowledge about who they are and what they are doing. When you do investigate and engage in more of a connection, they respond with ambiguous facts released with a certain air of mystification.

Aloof people might also imply that they know secrets no-one else knows, and even that these secrets reveal something that the pursuing person desperately needs to know. This pushes you to further your enquiries. It's a constant 'hide and seek' with them.

Their effort is to get your attention exclusively on them and for you to subconsciously allow them to have control of the relationship. It will give them the uplifting energy of your connection. You will never really feel like you know the person fully and will feel depleted around them.

Interactions with an Aloof person can be quite amusing, but their continual withdrawal will stress you out eventually.

You might ask, 'How was your weekend,' and receive only a brief, cryptic answer. They might say, 'Very good,' giving you no details. Asking a follow-up question yields an equally distant reply.

How can you tell whether the person you are interacting with is playing the Aloof game or just doesn't want to open up to you? Give up, walk off briefly, or just be silent. The Aloof person, who is actively pursuing the energy, will want to keep your connection. They will tend to give just a little more info to keep you interested, something such as, 'It was a great weekend, actually.' When you enquire more about it, they will seize control and go vague again or change the subject.

Quick Fix

Again, remember that most Aloof people do not do it on purpose; they almost feel like they don't want to burden you with their life, hence they are reserving their information for those most interested. That's the narrative they play in their head. There is a big chance that as children one or both of their parents didn't have time for them and the only way they could grab their attention would be by disappearing – throwing the parent into panic or enquiry. Only when the parent was enquiring about them did they feel like somebody cared.

If you want to break the Aloof's conscious **or** unconscious manipulation, express precisely how you feel about this interaction. Say something such as, 'Every time I try to get to know you or really share your life, I feel like I can never get a straight answer.' By 'naming the game' you will bring the manipulation (whether conscious or unconscious) to light. Just make sure you remain authentic to yourself and don't slip into your own manipulation, such as the 'interrogator', which is the natural partner game to the Aloof.

The Interrogator Manipulation

A more aggressive personality is the Interrogator. You know when you run into this style of manipulation because you suddenly feel criticized and begin to monitor your actions so that you feel less vulnerable. Usually the person playing such a game has learned to put you down (often under the disguise of being helpful) to seize control of the relationship. Subtle criticism forces you to lose confidence and to begin to look at yourself through the eyes of the Interrogator, giving the Interrogator power and energy, leaving you feeling depleted.

The Interrogator will pass cunning comments that could be about appearance, like, 'Don't you think you're wearing too much makeup for this occasion?' Or it could be about behavior: 'That was a really stupid thing to say.' It could even be about intelligence: 'I think that job is way out of your league.' It could be criticism in any shape or form. What it's really about is the completely manipulative Interrogator throwing you completely off balance so that they can take on the leadership role in the relationship.

All the good feelings and security that the manipulator gets from this relationship moves into the front of their mind and therefore into their consciousness. However, the victim in the relationship feels completely damaged and feels bad about themselves too. It can be described as a joined mind of the Interrogator and their victim. But how do you rise above this game being played by the Interrogator and bring the joined mind into balance?

Quick Fix

You need to name the game by saying exactly how you feel, for example, 'When I'm around you I feel like you are criticizing me the whole time.' This will stop the manipulation, as the Interrogator needs to deal with how you are feeling.

No doubt, the first answer you will get is that you are wrong. But stick to your guns and hold onto your newfound power. You don't want to become an Interrogator or an Aloof yourself, nor do you want to transfer all the energy to yourself so that you belittle the person.

Your remark will leave an imprint on the person, even if the Interrogator never admits the manipulation. What might really stop the Interrogator in their tracks is if others follow your example and uncover the manipulation too. You can only hope that they eventually get it. If, after you've confronted the Interrogator openly, you find you were wrong about their intentions and they were just trying to be helpful, don't worry, you have done what's necessary to bring your relationship into genuine truth and growth.

The Intimidator Manipulation

This is the most aggressive type of manipulation. The Intimidator scares you into complying with their control in the relationship. This is not someone to be messed with; they are dangerous and will often resort to violence to ensure that the game works.

How do you know if you're dealing with an Intimidator? You'll sense an air of aggression in their attitude and their mannerisms. They have normally grown up in an environment where they could only get attention by acting out in this way.

Quick Fix

This one is a little tricky as I am not sure it can be classified as a 'quick fix'. Just like with previous manipulations, honesty is definitely the best policy. You need to find subtle ways to 'name the game' with the Intimidator. You should consider your safety and use your judgment wisely. Occasionally the Intimidator will be in a relationship with a Poor Me who has learned to argue back submissively by guilt tripping or pleading. This is often the dynamic which makes people stay together in relationships that are either verbally abusive or violent. The only option out is to leave the relationship and seek shelter elsewhere.

Have you discovered which manipulation you personally use? It's not just other humans who play this game – you do it as well.

I found this a bit mind-blowing the first time I came across it. Having this knowledge not only will make you aware of how you tend to control others (and perhaps stop yourself) but will also give you the ability to release yourself from situations where you feel like you are being controlled. And it will help you build better relationships with others, as you will be aware of what you are doing.

Using words like:

'Are you trying to make me feel guilty?'

'Are you trying to make me feel insecure?'

All said with a smile in a 'light and joking' way, these are some of the most powerful words I have ever used to snap people out of their manipulations. They will often say, 'No, no, of course not,' and they will never try that on me again.

The Masks We Wear

Now, before we start judging ourselves and others around us, let's look a little deeper into why we have adopted those 'manipulations' and how they have been protecting us over the years.

As previously discussed, when you were born you were totally reliant on the people who raised you - your 'tribe'. Whoever your tribe was – whether it be one parent, two parents, foster carers, grandparents, teachers – it was all the grownups which had an impact on how you were raised.

As a child you can only know yourself by the feedback you get from your tribe. You want to know that you are as amazing as you think you are. You want to know that you matter, that you are lovable and accepted, and that your thoughts and feelings are important. As a child you need to know that when you are vulnerable you will be fully heard and not be shamed, shut down, judged, mocked or rejected. You are forever looking at people around you to validate yourself.

But that is not what happens in real life. In real life, your tribe needs you to be a certain way **before** you get their approval and love. And since most adults are (unconsciously) 'screwed up' themselves (by previous generations), you end up learning to not be yourself but **adapt** to please the tribe.

To you as a child, there are two things which are super important:

1. Your tribe is OK
2. You are OK

Unfortunately, the tribe is more important at that stage, as without them your survival is at risk – after all, if they are gone, who will give you food and water and shelter? At that age you were totally absorbed in your own world and desperately trying to fit in – this is why you **always** assumed responsibility and saw yourself as being at fault. Every time as a child you receive negative feedback through normal parenting, you interpret it as 'I am faulty'. **Every** time!

And because of this we develop different masks or personalities which not only shut down parts of our true self but are also necessary to keep you safe and keep the balance within your household.

Importantly, understand that you not only made those decisions **unconsciously** but also made them as a little child, when your context of the world was not yet developed. It's **not** your fault. This was the time where all you were doing was drawing a metaphorical 'map', or a blueprint, of how life should be and how to fit in. Your assumption was always that everything around you (family dysfunctions and all) was perfectly normal and, since you assumed you were 'wrong', you had to figure out how to BE.

Just look back to the way your tribe interacted when you were very young. Was your parents' relationship a superb example of what a great love relationship should look like? Was everything around you an example of perfect life? If there were glitches, stresses and disorder, that is exactly what has been recorded in your own blueprint and you see as **normal, perfect** and the way **it should be**. It's you who had to adjust.

These adjustments lead to a shutdown of certain emotions, which in later life can lead to dysfunctions and feeling 'fake', 'not fulfilled' or a 'product of compromise'. In fact, in stronger cases it can lead to confusion, feeling lost, anxiety and depression.

When you were told to behave in a certain way, punished if you didn't, when you said or did something you were shamed, shut down, judged, mocked or rejected in any way, you automatically associated those actions or feelings with being bad. All it took was one experience and your powerful computer, a.k.a. your subconscious mind, shut down this part of you. You would do anything to avoid those feelings again. And, the more intense the experiences, the bigger the shutdown.

Were you allowed to speak up? Cry? Be angry? Sad? Stressed? Frustrated? If any of these emotions were frowned upon or punished, there is a whole lot of you right now that is hiding in the shadows – possibly behind this beautiful mask of 'I am OK'.

If, as a child, the person you looked up to didn't have time for you, that was translated as **abandonment**, which simply gets encoded as 'I'm not lovable'. As you look back at it now as an adult, you understand parents had to work, some divorced or had to go on a trip. As an adult you might understand it, but guess what? That's NOT what your brain coded! What got coded is: **Abandonment! 'I am not lovable'!**

Just one serious incident like this as a child can later in life lead to a person having either superiority or inferiority problems. One child turns around and says, 'Stuff you – I don't need love,' and becomes overly reliant and emotionally detached; another child will always feel inferior and become a people pleaser to 'win' their love back. Either way, both will develop serious intimacy problems (see the next chapter on how it plays out in relationships).

If you were rewarded for acting a certain way, you learned that this is what is required to be loved. Perfectionism, overachievement, power and a lot of things the media would like us to associate with 'success' are also learned survival tactics and often take a toll on us eventually. Behind the mask of a perfectionist and someone super-successful on the surface is just a child who had super-high hoops to jump through in order to feel loved.

Below are some triggers which you might or might not have experienced as a child. Any of these feelings would have created pathways in your subconscious mind and developed your current character:

- Unworthy or worthless
- Disapproved of, invalidated or rejected
- Not listened to or understood
- Invisible to grownups
- Unloved, not cared about or wanted
- Insulted, disparaged, disrespected, distrusted, devalued or discounted
- Aggressed against, taken advantage of, betrayed
- Inadequate, defective, incompetent, behind the curve, inferior or looked down upon, unacceptable
- Slow, stupid, foolish or silly, contemptible
- Dishonorable or cowardly
- Embarrassed or humiliated
- Weak, helpless or defenseless
- Undeserving of time, attention or recognition

- Like a failure; 'loser'
- Guilty, shameful or a bad person generally

All of the above feelings a child might have experienced (a lot of them unintentionally inflicted via reverse psychology) will automatically be written into their coding so as to be avoided at all costs in the future. A big WARNING sign goes up and any situation which could get you anywhere close to those experiences is avoided.

No child ever wants to be shamed, shut down, judged, mocked, rejected, feel unloved or abandoned. You will automatically adjust your behaviors to avoid those situations experienced as a child by putting on a mask. That mask is a way of being – allowing you safely to fit in within your tribe. Over the years, this mask will blend into your personality and, as much as you might enjoy your personality right now (each one has its great positives), there will be parts of you which have been shut down. The thing is, you don't ever realize they have been shut down because you only know what you know; you feel like you have always been that way. The only little giveaway is an emptiness you might feel inside you – the feeling of untapped potential.

Here are some examples of masks we take on to adjust to our tribe:

The People Pleaser – a constantly judged child who learns that the only way to get love is by doing stuff for other people. They are the super-nice ones. They will go to desperate lengths to please people around them. Their sense of identity is based on what others think and their need to be constantly validated. They are easily influenced by others, and they find it incredibly hard to make decisions or say no to others. They will constantly ask the advice of friends, family, doctors, experts, co-workers and mentors because they lack strong foundations.

The Rebel – the only way this child could get any attention was by doing the opposite of what they were told. It's a child who, after being ignored, abused or rejected, has their defense mechanism kick in and they decide to 'be different'. Being 'different' is what gets them noticed and helps them to feel significant. They learn to reject love, as in their world love requires too much of a sacrifice. They also tend to be determined not to follow parents' footsteps and question authority.

The Superstar – oh, parents have to have bragging rights, right? The child only gets noticed when the tribe could use the child as an example of their (parents') achievement. A huge amount of pressure is placed on the child and love is withdrawn unless they perform well.

The Superhero – the tough one; reliable, saves everybody, in charge, never fazed by anything, and pretends to be strong even when everything is falling apart inside. This was usually developed by a child who had to be the rescuer for one of the parents or a sibling when the other parent was emotionally or physically absent – the child was expected to be the designated 'grownup'.

The Sunshine – overly positive, everything is great, life is perfect. This is a child who was not allowed to say negative things about what was happening at home. Negative emotions were discouraged or punished. Silence was golden and superficial perceptions were everything.

The Intellectual/Perfectionist – some people unconsciously pursue intellectual perfectionism as a defense against 'not belonging'. If everything is done right, then their world can't fall apart. The child probably got a lot of praise for being 'smart' or 'getting good grades', and this importance was the only way the tribe was 'proud of them'. Not getting good grades was punishable. Although getting praise for being 'perfect' might bring occasional relief, the perfectionist is always at the mercy of something going wrong or someone being smarter, and therefore lives in a constant state of anxiety. Their stubbornness, obsessiveness and lack of trust build a barrier between them and their loved ones.

The Little Soldier – overly judged, only got rewarded for doing things right and obeying strict rules, thus becoming super-rigid themselves. They can't make decisions because of the fear of doing it wrong. They become overly judgmental. They grow up to have huge self-belief issues.

The Little Princess – a show-off; constantly complimented for beauty and external features; life has to be perfect and beautiful otherwise they are not good enough for the tribe. They must be the best and can throw a tantrum to prove it. You can see lots of these humans on Instagram these days.

The Cool Guy – on the outside, this person seems to have mastered whatever it takes to stay cool, calm and collected. Anger was unacceptable or punished in their tribe. The child grows up to be externally unfazed by conflict or chaos but, beneath the surface, one of two things happens. The bottled-up emotions result in either a nervous breakdown or serious addictions, or they periodically snap at people who are inferior to them, which to onlookers seems like an absolute overkill. This in turn makes them hate themselves for losing their cool, and so the spiral goes on.

The Bully – there is a fair share of bullies wherever we look. They can control you through subtle and gentle exploitation so that you see things through their eyes. Or they can be aggressive, and even physical. Outwardly they seem confident due to the way they express their opinions and order, but inwardly they are super-insecure. One of their greatest wants in life is to be respected, and they will break the rules of accepted behavior to get that esteem. Their aggressive behavior is driven by self-doubt. They have an obsessive need to be right, which unfortunately comes at the cost of those around them and their feelings.

The Introvert – the timid person or introvert is deathly afraid of failure and rejection. They would much rather feel the pains of loneliness than risk not being liked. Like the perfectionists, they are so afraid of making a mistake that they refuse to challenge themselves. They blush easily, get embarrassed easily and don't say much for fear of saying the wrong thing. As you can imagine, this was developed as a protection mechanism from being overly criticized and/or punished.

The Social Butterfly – although they are the life of the party, the social butterfly is innately lonely. They compensate for feelings of insecurity with their gift of the gab and small talk. They have many acquaintances but few, if any, real friends. Although their calendar is packed full of social events, their life lacks meaning. They keep their conversations superficial because deeper dialogues may expose their anxiety or shed their confident persona.

The Self-Basher – they seriously play the victim due to feeling totally unworthy and insecure, all the while showing a negative view of themselves. Sadly, they harm themselves first just to stay out of harm's way. More than likely they insult themselves and put themselves down to protect themselves from any disasters that might be heading their way like a shitstorm. Their defense mechanism is self-criticism and through this they avoid any risk of intimacy.

The Grumpy Cat – being a jerk is an intimidation factor, which is overcompensating for a lack of confidence, just like a bully. Any of their macho behavior, bullying and aggression are often attempts to protect their fragile self-esteem. They've been hurt, and this mask protects them from being embarrassed, hurt or rejected again for whatever reason. This mask is usually a sign that someone is lonely, scared, fearful, and desperately wants respect. But, ironically, wearing this mask only isolates them more from others.

The Scapegoat – parents or siblings constantly blame their incompetency on a child. After a while, the child will volunteer to have the blame placed on them. In fact, often the scapegoat will create problems to take their tribe's focus away from the real family issues by becoming rebellious, defiant and rude – often getting themselves in trouble with the law and illegal substances.

The Designated Patient – parents paid more attention and gave more love when the child got sick. This sent a signal to the child's subconscious mind that in order to receive love one needs to get sick. And, since your subconscious mind is in charge of one trillion cells in your body, what you ask for you shall receive. If your survival and receipt of love depends on your being unwell, your subconscious mind will do anything to make sure you are always a 'patient'.

The Surrogate Spouse – one parent was either emotionally or physically absent and the child was expected to be the physical or emotional support for the parent, often exposed to emotions they were too young to deal with. Depending on the severity of this burden, to a child, love often gets associated with huge sacrifice and is unconsciously avoided in older years, leading to intimacy issues in relationships.

The Comedian – this is the one who will always 'lighten the mood' through humor. They're the child who tried to balance the sadness in the tribe. Although superficially a positive attribute, using humor as a defense mechanism can and does prevent intimacy. Sarcasm especially tends to be rooted in pain and is not without consequences. The comedian tells a joke to avoid sincere discussions, to keep conversations from getting too real or deep. Uncomfortable with conflict, the child will charm their way out of confrontation. The comedy serves as a protective shield, making it hard to allow anyone in – leaving the person feeling lonely.

The Control Freak – uses order and power to achieve a sense of security. By making sure everything is in its proper place, they relieve their fear of the unknown, of ambiguity, of uncertainty. A mother hen, the control freak won't let anyone out of their sight and assumes responsibility for all those around them, even when they don't want to be cared for. They become unraveled when anyone deviates from the plan.

These are examples of only some of the masks we wear, and I am sure you can add many more characters to this list. Some of us have a blend of more than one – after all, the subconscious mind is all about custom-making the best protection mechanisms possible.

Have you been able to pick up on the way your subconscious adjusted to your tribe?

It's important to note that all of us have lived a different childhood. Just look at you and your sibling/s. I have always wondered why my sister and I have turned out so differently. After all, we had the same parents and a similar childhood. I was always the good child overachiever and she was the rebel overachiever. We were both super-competitive and successful in our own right, yet our approach to everything was different.

The reason? Most of the time, if a certain mask is already taken by the older sibling, the younger one takes on a different role so that balance is achieved. If one of the siblings was the superstar in one area and parents think the best of them, there is not much point competing. You either become a hero at something totally different that your sibling cannot do, become a rebel, become a designated patient...or, if nothing else works, you might just laugh it off by becoming a comedian. Look back at the tribe you grew up in and you will soon see how you had to become the person you did to fit in like a puzzle piece into that tribe. You would do anything to keep the balance.

Dr John Bradshaw uses an example of a baby's mobile with soft toys hanging from it – the pieces need to balance each other for the mobile to work and, when they do, it looks like a happy, healthy structure working in harmony. Using this example to illustrate family structure, you had to take on a role within **your** tribe which would balance the 'mobile'. This wasn't your choice – this was plain survival. This was done unconsciously by your subconscious mind at an age where you had no idea of the context, no choice and no ability to reason.

Even more powerful is that ever since your first incident of that 'rejection' or 'toxic shame' you experienced, whether you were one or two or five years old, your mind not only defaulted to a role but has been collecting data to prove that the mask you are wearing is the correct one.

Over time, with the help of confirmation bias, you have attracted only those experiences which confirm your mask to be the right choice for you. Your mind has converted that mask into a character you have been playing all your life. That character is often referred to as an 'ego'. Just imagine an ego is a character which protects the real you from the outside world – like a big, loving but way overprotective sibling hiding the real you behind them.

With millions of bits of information flying at you every single second, your mind will filter through and record **only** what's useful and important. It is crucial for you to understand that, with confirmation bias, your mind will collect files upon files to support why this mask is your best protection mechanism.

As the mask constantly protects you from hurt and ensures your tribal 'mobile' remains balanced, as you get older your mask literally takes over and you develop it into a personality/ego. Your mask becomes so 'stuck' to your face that your true self gets lost. You cling onto your ego more and more, and soon you start to believe that this is who you really are.

Stuck On You – Attachment Theory

The mask you adopted as a child by your super-helpful subconscious mind gets even messier when you start getting into relationships. Chances are the amount of love you felt as a child (during your coding years – up to the age of seven) and the blueprint you have coded from what you saw growing up (what a 'perfect relationship' looked like) will determine how you will 'tackle' your own relationships moving forward.

If you, at any stage of your coding years as a child, felt abandoned you are on a path of self-destruction. You will always look for something that will fit your original blueprint and prove that, if you divert from your mask, you will get abandoned again! Ouch!

Have you ever met someone who was very familiar and you hit it off with them really well? Initially? Well, that 'familiarity' is just something that reminds your subconscious of your original blueprint. You will be attracted to things you're familiar with. And then, if you experienced rejection or abandonment in the past, here comes history repeating itself! Your confirmation bias will again and again prove itself right that you are 'unlovable' so that the mask you carry will be more and more reinforced!

Now, before you despair too much about this, wait! There is a way out of that pattern. We will discuss the 'escape' from the original coding in the upcoming chapters. But first, for a better understanding of where you are at, let's check out 'attachment theory', famous in psychology (Bowlby and Ainsworth 1950s).

Below you will find four different ways you or your partner might respond to a 'romantic' relationship. Depending on how your subconscious mind registered love and vulnerability in your coding years, here is how it plays out in your adulthood.

The Avoidant Type

The Avoidant Type is extremely independent, self-sufficient, confident but quite uncomfortable with deep connection. They are commitment-phobes who escape any intimate situations. They often date on a very superficial level. Have you ever met somebody who ghosted you after a few dates?

They often have a lifestyle that allows them to avoid deeper relationships, such as being workaholics or super-busy individuals. They tend to invest much more in the beginning phases of a relationship than in the later phases – this way they can enjoy the exciting aspects of relationships while escaping when that deeper connection threatens to form. They can be a lot of fun and make for very charming daters but disappointing long-term partners, often just simply disappearing.

Avoidants often use humor to quickly diffuse situations that might become too emotional. It's one of their most effective tactics because their fear of intimacy is well hidden behind jokes and sarcasm.

Their avoidance can often be funny in a very irreverent way, which makes us think that they've got everything under control. They will also use that biting sense of humor to control others when they begin to open up to them – they're prone to shame any sort of display of emotion and return to the limited connection that they are much more comfortable with.

They often complain about being 'suffocated' if someone gets closer to them. In a relationship, they want their partner – but not so much their partner's presence. If their significant other isn't near, they'll miss them, but when they return the Avoidant may start to feel stifled immediately. There are always a lot of mixed signals.

Like all attachment types, the Avoidant is created in the first seven years of their life. Something occurred that made the Avoidant associate connection with pain, hence the tremendous unconscious effort that they exert to escape it. A typical story is that one or both parents were physically present but emotionally unavailable.

People with an Avoidant attachment style often self-sabotage themselves out of blossoming romance. Because of the fear of being abandoned, they will find fault and walk away from the relationship first. This is their attempt to make sure they will never go through abandonment again. They don't realize that by using those protection mechanisms they are sabotaging themselves and they recreate the very thing that they try to avoid.

When the relationship comes to an end, they often persuade themselves that they didn't really have emotions for that person anyway. They also often move onto their next partnership to prove how unaffected they are.

The Anxious Type

The total opposite to the Avoidant, the Anxious Type craves connection and fears its loss. They are often nervous and stressed about their relationship. They need constant reassurance and affection from their partner.

They are often in relationships or hopping from one to another. For an Anxious Type, being without a cherished connection can feel like dying. They often describe it that way, saying, 'You're my everything,' or, 'When I think of not being with you, I can't breathe.'

Unconsciously, the Anxious Type sometimes uses the pain of being without their loved one to control the person they're in a relationship with. They make the other person fear their own suffering, sometimes so much so that they might not end the relationship even if it is failing. Other times the Anxious Type might literally threaten self-harm. The problem with the Anxious Type is that they project an idealized image onto the object of their affection. Their low self-image can blind them to the flaws of others, making them willing to change anything just to be close to that person.

Unfortunately, the Anxious Type has a low self-image, which also makes them suspect that the perfect object of their desire could never really want to be with them; not for long anyway. Even when in a relationship with such a person they tend to cling on tightly but eventually all that clinging turns to suspicion and jealousy, and they drive people away, confirming what they've suspected all along.

Like the Avoidant, the reason the Anxious Type is both needy of attention and expecting of abandonment goes back to childhood. Obviously there can be many factors that cause this, but the loss of a cherished caretaker at a young age can be one.

The Fearful Type

This type is very rare compared with other types. Only a small percentage of the population qualifies as the Fearful (or Anxious-Avoidant) Type, and they typically have a multitude of other emotional problems in other areas of their life (i.e. substance abuse, depression, etc.)

They can be unpredictable, and they find ways to sabotage the very things that they seem to want most. A main attribute of the Fearful Type is that they bounce between anxious behavior like people pleasing and then avoidance behavior like 'ghosting' due to fear of abandonment.

The Fearful Type craves, yet is uncomfortable with, the affection that comes in a relationship, which makes them lash out unpredictably at the people they care about the most. If you've ever known someone who can't seem to find a stable relationship no matter whom they date, who becomes more violent as they get closer to someone, you may have witnessed a Fearful Type in action.

The Fearful Type has often experienced childhood trauma, which may have included verbal, physical or sexual abuse. They may have felt that they had no-one whom they could rely on for love.

The Fearful Type has the most robust defense mechanisms because in their experience vulnerability means ultimate pain. In those rare emotional moments when the vulnerability is threatening to expose itself, you can see just about every defense mechanism under the sun kicking in.

Now, if this seems like you, you will find this book very beneficial as it will teach you that, regardless of what you have been through, the coding you inherited is definitely reversible.

And the painful experiences can be harnessed to give you immense strength and ability to help others once you follow the process in this book.

The Secure Type

Unfortunately, we don't see a whole lot of the Secure Type in romantic movies because they don't tend to be very dramatic. They don't cling or run because, unlike all the other Attachment Types, the relationships of the Secure Type are not driven by fear. That isn't to say that they don't feel fear; they simply trust that they have the strength to deal with the inevitable heartache that comes from deeper connections.

The Secure Type can trust others to see them in vulnerable moments because of an unconscious belief that they can open up without immediately being burned for it. They're also comfortable in conflict because they aren't afraid of abandonment when they disagree with someone. They tend to do so in a calm manner.

When it comes to working with others, they don't have a one-size-fits-all solution. They don't need to be mindlessly independent or fearfully group oriented; they can treat each situation separately and decide whether their goals are best achieved by working alone or by relying on others.

The common thread with the Secure Type is that they are not re-enacting their childhood trauma, so they can treat each new relationship as it is. They're focused not just on whether there is a connection but on the quality of that connection. They keep the good ones and discard the bad.

It's worth noting that you don't necessarily have to fall into one category. Depending on the severity of your childhood experiences, your conditioning might be mostly Secure with tendencies towards either Anxious or Avoidant.

In long-term relationships we can attract same types, but, as you can imagine, we often attract the opposite. If both partners are Secure, the relationship will flourish. If, however, we tend to be more Avoidant, the only person we will attract who is willing to stick around long enough is the Anxious Type. These relationships usually result in either unhappy marriages, affairs or eventual divorces.

Though two Anxious Types may start with a great love story, it usually will end up in constant jealousy and insecurities, and they won't be able to cope with the pressure of a long-term relationship.

The Avoidant Type is also attracted to their own type because of their strong confidence levels. Although they make epic love affairs, their relationships don't last, as both of them will be constantly proving to each other how emotionally unaffected they are and how little they care (which could be totally opposite to how they actually feel).

The love affair soon turns into a power struggle as they easily lose connection. The only way to create a great lasting relationship is for both partners to recognize where they are on their power struggle spectrum and then work at getting themselves back to a balanced or secure state.

Bruce H. Lipton Ph.D. has written an amazing book called 'The Honeymoon Effect'. I highly, highly recommend reading it!

One of the most brilliant analogies Bruce uses is chemistry. Even if you are not a chemistry buff you will enjoy this comparison. I will try to simplify it for you...

Most of the atoms on the periodic table create chemical bonds – all except for six referred to as 'noble gases'. The reason why atoms create 'chemistry' is simple. Their structure has protons (positive charges) and electrons (negative charges). The distribution of those is uneven and they therefore create unbalance when they are spinning, like towels in a dryer that get stuck on one side, so the atoms look for other atoms which are unbalanced and spinning in the opposite direction and bond with them so that their spinning evens out.

This is what we do in relationships. Our subconscious mind tends to find a partner that complements and balances our unobserved imbalances. The partnership might drive you crazy, but you feel like you need it desperately to be 'happy'. One 'wobbly' personality attracts another 'wobbly' personality until they form a 'bond' and then they seem to spin better together. This is why so many people stay in unhappy relationships or, worse, attract abusive relationships. Even though they might not like it, they feel as though they need it.

Lipton explains that in order to attract an amazing partner you need to become like a 'noble gas' atom (as mentioned, there are only six of them on the periodic table): be balanced and happy to 'spin on your own'. Once you have aligned your conscious and unconscious minds, you are no longer a sodium atom desperately looking for a chlorine atom; you don't need another element to be balanced.

Also important and worth remembering is: every relationship 'has four minds'. Both people in the relationship each have a conscious mind and an unconscious mind; that's why relationships can get so confusing. When you first meet your partner, you are very present with them and everything seems unbelievably incredible. It's all music, sunshine and rainbows. That's because you both are enjoying each other's presence on a conscious level. You are fun, you are creative and you are on top of the world. But then something happens which triggers your subconscious mind to 'kick in'. Your walls go up and your ego tries to rescue you from the possibility of getting hurt. This could be triggered by something said or unsaid...a grimace, a behavior, a sound – literally anything that is stored in your memory bank which has in the past been associated with something negative. Most of the time it has **nothing** to do with your partner but, rather, with your interpretation of an incident that happened in the past. That's when you get that 'gut feeling' – which is just code for 'I've seen something like this in the past' – and, **bang,** walls go up and the 'honeymoon is over'.

It's **so crucial** to realize that you have a choice.

The aligning of the conscious and unconscious minds and becoming a Secure Type simply means becoming your authentic self and removing the mask you have developed as a child. Holding onto the mask is a recipe for an **unfulfilled** life as your **true** identity gets lost behind it and can create feelings of emptiness.

As the years go by, you may feel there is something missing in your life. You feel like you are stuck playing a performance for the outside world. You start asking, 'Is this all there is to life? How much longer can I keep up the appearances of being perfect, being cool and having my "shit" together?'

You don't understand why you feel this way, but you are tired of the performance. There's this unexplainable hollowness inside you. You have long forgotten that there are parts of you that have been shut down. You are afraid to look in there because in the past it was always associated with pain – that's why your subconscious disconnected it in the first place. Your joy, your spontaneity, your sense of self-love has been shut down in order to survive and conform to your mask, which has been created to protect you. The more you hold onto your mask, the more you become like a deflated ball in search of external stimuli to fill that painful void inside.

Some people try to fill that void with career success, with chasing the money and getting rich. Some try to fill it with being more perfect: getting perfect homes, beautiful partners, fancy brands and shiny cars. Some through titles and education and a feeling of 'being super-intelligent'.

Some people chase popularity, desirability and beauty by trying to fill the void with 'likes' on social media. Some chase it through crime as it makes them feel powerful. Some people try to fill the void with dopamine hits through sex, drugs or rock and roll. Some get their kick through fast cars or extreme sports. Or through buying the newest trends or perhaps collecting some stuff. Or through association with famous people. Some through having big families. And the list goes on…

But the truth is more painful than this: no matter how much you try to have the external world 'fill you up', it will never work! We all know of rich, funny, smart or famous people who are terribly miserable – filling up via external stimuli is not how you fill the void.

Chasing those things to prop you up is like trying to find gold at the end of a rainbow. It's a perverted illusion marketing companies rely on to sell you stuff you don't need. It's a carrot you chase for the rest of your life only to finally realize in your dying hour that it has been nothing more than a lie!

Your true self doesn't want more fame, attention and success – our ego, the mask we wear, does! It's conditioned to believe that the only way it can protect you from shame is by making you super-successful so that people can notice and admire you.

Chasing success, by the way, is no different from a dog chasing a ball: as soon as you bring it back to the owner, the ball gets thrown again, and again, and again. I am using this as a metaphor, of course, but have you ever seen how the dog associates his happiness with getting the ball? Well, your subconscious mind has just trained you to think that the only way you will be happy is by achieving certain goals which are associated with fame, attention and success. And since there will **always** be people who might seem more successful or famous or 'steal' your current spotlight – guess what? If you get roped into this belief you will spend the rest of your life 'chasing the balls' your subconscious throws at you – and, the more you chase them, the farther the next ball will land. Your life will be no more than an exhausting pursuit of a mirage.

Your true self doesn't want to avoid intimacy – it craves it. The subconscious, however, has associated love with the sacrifice of having to put others' needs first – the ego is protecting you from that. Unless you learn to pull down your mask and get rid of your protective walls, you will never experience true intimacy.

Intimacy, by the way, is not sex and pleasure, as many confuse it with. If you break down the actual word, you will get 'IN-TO-ME-I–SEE'. Intimacy is the ability of being truly yourself with someone and being loved for who you truly are without the 'mask'. Unfortunately, the original programing has associated love with co-dependency, and you see it as having to give up your freedom – your subconscious avoids it at all costs. Intimacy has also often been associated with emotional or physical abandonment – your subconscious assumes all intimacy will lead to that, hence it avoids it at all costs. Even if it means leaving your true self forever unfulfilled, your subconscious mind has not been designed to take that risk.

Your true self doesn't want to procrastinate. It wants to experience life, be spontaneous and adventurous. If you find yourself procrastinating, your ego is just trying to protect you from shame and the feeling of not being good enough – it's therefore stopping you from trying new things, talking to new people or experiencing life in a different way.

The same goes for vulnerability.

Your protective ego always hides you from being vulnerable. It doesn't want to expose you to any potential situations, which in the past caused pain. We were never really encouraged to develop our own unique selves but we were molded to fit into our environment. As it was super important for us to fit in and uphold the balance of our tribes, we had our personal boundaries lost in the process. Our needs were completely sacrificed. This is why when we become adults we don't even know how to be. We are expected to be vulnerable in relationships with others, yet we have this massive warning sign in our minds telling us to be guarded.

This is why we experience so much emotional pain as adults. On the outside we walk around with a happy face, yet on the inside we have this well-hidden sense of lacking something or incompleteness. Sometimes this is represented as a constant feeling of not being worthy or good enough, and sometimes this is experienced as an intense craving as well as wanting and needing.

Those who default to feeling not good enough will become people pleasers and spend their life putting others first, constantly worrying and imagining worst-case scenarios.

Those with a more overachieving nature will deal with this incompleteness by trying to get the outside world to fill them up. They will start looking for things to identify with. They do everything in their power to get possessions, money, success, control, recognition, or a special relationship, basically in an attempt to feel good about themselves. This fills that void and makes them feel more whole. For a little while.

The most common form of gratification and identity has to do with possessions, the type of work you do, social status, recognition, knowledge and education, physical appearance, special abilities, relationships, family history, belief systems, and often also political, nationality, racial and other collective identifications. None of these are you.

Soon enough you find it doesn't matter how much you accumulate – the deep bottomless pit is still there. This is where trouble comes knocking on your door, as you can't fool yourself anymore.

You can't be fully at ease if your ego is running your mind. Being at ease or fulfilled becomes ridiculously hard, except for those fleeting moments when you get what you want and your craving has been fulfilled momentarily.

The ego's self-derived sense of itself needs to always identify with external stimulus, like a hamster constantly running on a wheel. It needs to be guarded and fed on a constant basis. It can be completely exhausting.

The constant chase or worry often ends with an emotional breakdown, when you know you can no longer keep up with your ego. The word 'depressed' is often used to describe a person who is emotionally broken. What's interesting, however, is that the word 'depressed', if you look at it differently, is just your soul telling you that you need DEEP REST. You need a break from the character you have been playing as it is not authentically who you really are. Your inner voice is telling you that the character you have developed is not congruent with your true self. You just need to rest it.

The ego and the subconscious mind are an amazing super-powerful computer and have served you well to get to where you are today. It protected you as a child from pain, shame, judgment and abandonment.

Unfortunately, the flipside to this protection is that it has automatically associated anything that could truly fulfill you with being a risk not worth taking, either sending you on a chase of things that don't even matter or 'forbidding you' from getting out of your comfort zone.

Ponder a little about where you are right now in life. Has that mask served you well? Do you feel truly fulfilled? Do you feel like you are being your authentic self? If the answer is yes – fantastic!

If, however, you feel that there is a bit of a void inside you – read on! I'll show you how you can get out of your current matrix (i.e. your subconscious programing) and recreate a pathway to a better, more fulfilling life – a life which keeps the parts of you that have celebrated your true self and which re-plugs in those dormant parts of you that have been hidden behind a protective ego.

PART 2
Awakening

There are lots of other examples of how our self-learned programs have taken over our thinking, and the more you dive into the studies of human psychology the more you will realize that 95% of what you do every day is simply run on autopilot by your conditioned mind (Szegedy-Maszak 2005) with your customized Siri calling the shots!

Your mind has been taken over by a computer program. And here is the kicker: it made you believe it's you! It thinks it's smarter than you and is happy to control you for the rest of your life! The mask which was initially designed to protect you so you can fit easily into your tribe is now running your every move – you are on cruise control of your subconscious mind. Welcome to your Matrix!

The only thing that threatens its current programing, which has or has not been running smoothly for all these years, is your personal growth.

Personal growth is something that is not easily accepted by the subconscious mind because it's **not** aligned with what it already knows, and it therefore constantly rejects new ideas. Have you ever read a great book and tried implementing things, just to return to the status quo shortly after? Yep, that's your mind acknowledging that, yes, you are conscious of the idea now, you '**know**', but your computer system spat it out because it didn't match its original programing, and therefore there will be no change in habit. After all, if **knowing things** would be sufficient to change, nobody in their right mind would smoke cigarettes, take drugs or eat junk food we all know makes us fat.

We all KNOW that in order to keep fit all you have to do is eat healthily and move your body – yet we are not all shining examples of 'that knowledge'. Knowledge is not enough – and neither is strong will, which, incidentally, only works like an elastic band: the more you force yourself via strong will, the more painful is the return to the status quo. The dominance of the subconscious mind is insanely powerful!

The only way you can make permanent changes in your life is to rewrite your programing, which, once you establish what you really want out of life, I will guide you through in further chapters. You will be able to keep all the good traits that your subconscious has developed and reprogram those that do not serve you anymore. Just like an upgrade on your PC, we will override the outdated parts of your blueprint for life.

Before we take that deep dive into programing, however, there is one more thing you will need to grasp. Now, this is pretty crucial, so pay attention – it's a paradigm shift that will help you realize that our fundamental understanding of how the mind works is, simply put, backwards!

If you thought that being controlled by your subconscious was interesting, **this** will add another dimension to your understanding.

There are three universal principles which we all knew existed but somehow never really put them together until the 1970s, when the late Sydney Banks first introduced them to the world as a way of understanding the human experience. These three principles are as fundamental as the law of gravity. Whether you believe in gravity or not, you will end up on your ass from time to time! The law does not care if you are a believer. And neither do these three principles of human experience.

The Principle Of The Universal Mind

This time, I'm not talking about our 'conditioned, programmed, subconscious mind', which we have been referring to so far. I am talking about the intelligence and energy behind all life – the energy we are all connected to.

Whether or not you are a religious or spiritual person, or whether you are a science buff, you know in your heart of hearts that there is something bigger, something unexplainable out there that has created and is powering this world we live in. The energy that gets a flower growing from a seed, an oak tree from an acorn and a human being from a fun date...the 'thing' that, regardless of whether you believe in it or not, you trust!

You trust it will wake you up tomorrow, you trust it will let you breathe and exist. You trust it will give you energy to get through life and trust that it will turn night into day and spring into summer – that's the Universal Mind I am talking about. It's the energy that makes the world exist and ensures that life continues.

You know it's inside you. It's the creative force that sometimes comes up with some brilliant ideas. It's the innate intelligence that created this exquisite world. It's by far the biggest asset we humans possess and one that is most underutilized!

The Universal Mind is ever present, constant and dependable. It is a bit like the Wi-Fi connection to your powerful computer.

It's the driving force behind everything and it knows everything.

The only way to access this Universal Mind is through either quietening the conscious mind via meditation or truly grasping the concept that your conscious mind has two channels. One is the **active channel** that thinks and talks (through our internal voice – Siri), but there is also a **receiver channel**, which connects you with the Universal Mind.

Most humans only utilize their conscious mind to retrieve messages from the stored memory. Connecting to the Universal Mind is like suddenly connecting a powerful PC to the Internet. Suddenly your mind is **so much smarter**!!!!

The reason you are not in tune with the real-deal Universal Mind constantly is that the subconscious mind, or program (a.k.a. Matrix), has taken over and is running your life 95% of the time.

Before you despair that your mind has been hijacked by a computer program, relax – it's super-fast and designed for your protection. Let's face it, you don't really want to be wasting your creativity on running your internal organs or having to re-learn reading and writing every day.

It is important, though, that you realize that those two mind channels exist and you can therefore tune into the Universal Mind and figure out what self-learning programs, beliefs and habits have been installed in your 'computer'. It will also allow you to recognize any 'faulty' blocks and beliefs that have been slowing you down, and to remove them in order to live to your full potential. More on that in the next chapter...

But it's crucial to recognize that without the Universal Mind you would not exist. In fact, nothing would exist.

The Principle Of Consciousness

The Principle of Consciousness is our awareness of life. It's our instinctive capability to experience life as a conscious being. Without being conscious, your life would not exist as you know it – you would have a bunch of thoughts passing unnoticed through your mind.

Consciousness is your ability to make sense of your thinking. It's your internal 'interpreter' – a.k.a. customized Siri – and it tells you whether the kind of experience you are having is good or bad, helpful or unhelpful, pleasurable or painful. It helps us to make sense of it all.

The Principle Of Thought

We live inside a world of thoughts. They come and go as they please, random as heck and sometimes annoying. Each thought comes attached to a feeling. It's like a two-sided coin: one side has a thought on it, the other has a feeling. If you were to close your eyes for 20 seconds, you'd discover that there is no particular order to the way thoughts arrive. Now, most of us know that. But what many don't know is that each thought is a **made-up thing**. It's not real!

Let me give you an example. If I were to say the word 'love', your interpretation of love and mine would be totally different. That's because your conditioned mind runs back to its 'filing cabinet' in its memory and fetches all the files you stored on the subject – therefore giving you a meaning and a feeling associated with this word. And, since your experience of love is different to mine, we have a different perception of that particular word.

If I were to say the word 'money', your concept of and feelings about money would be different to mine. Your idea of money is made up of **your** own thinking – just random thoughts that add up to your idea of money.

In fact, if you ponder further, you will find that every topic you put forward will attract a bunch of other thoughts that will create definition and meaning for you, and they will be totally or slightly different to mine or your neighbors'.

This all relates back to all the information that your memory – that cute little container – has stored over the years about every object, subject and abstract idea.

If you can grasp that concept, you will understand that **everybody's** definition of **reality** is different, even when looking at the same thing. You could have a million people reading this book right now and everybody's perception of it will be totally different. That's because everybody's reality **is different**. Which begs the question: what is **real**? The answer is simple – there is no such thing as common 'REALITY'!

Your subconscious mind creates its own map of what is happening outside by coding only what's relevant to it. Just imagine if you were driving through a totally new city and had to create a map of what you saw outside the window as you drove past. You would place on your map only things which are noticeable, relevant and maybe useful for the future. But there is no chance you could ever capture everything. Your mind works in the same way. It memorizes only the things which are relevant to your current beliefs. So the outside world we all live in might be the same **but** everybody has a different map in their heads. Everybody!

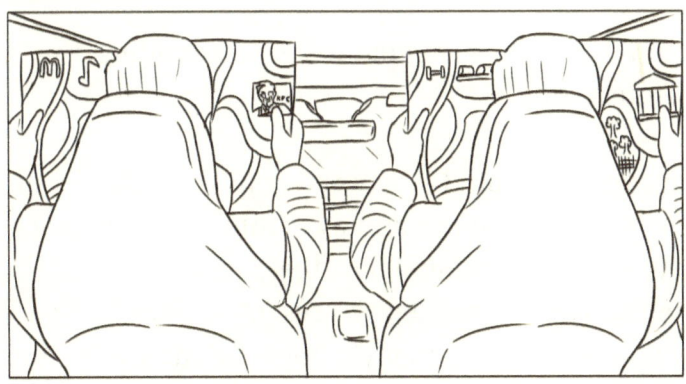

The Principle of Thought extends even further. Not only is your subconscious mind creating your own version of reality – it also **time travels**. It constantly throws your thoughts into either the future or past tense, leaving you rarely enjoying the **now**. It's a brilliant trick to keep you engaged in the 'game'.

Let me give you an example. Just imagine you are stuck in traffic, waiting at the traffic lights. Your thoughts wander to the conversation you had with your friend yesterday about the trip you are planning next year. Mmm, it'll be nice to get away, a tropical destination, the feeling of the sun on your face, the taste of pina coladas by the pool, the Latin music in the background, the laughter of people around you, the...

'Beep, beep' goes a car behind you – you snap out of your thoughts, realizing your light just turned green and some impatient driver behind you is shouting at you to move.

What you have just experienced is **traveling in time** to the past conversation with your friend and then into the future event you are planning. But in reality you were stuck at traffic lights in a present moment. So, even though you were 'experiencing' your past and your future, you never really left your car.

Or, should I say, in fact you were just reading this book? Hmmm, interesting...

Your subconscious mind is extremely powerful and will often hijack your conscious awareness from being present. The minute you start thinking about the past or wander into the future tense, you are no longer present in your body. It's like 'the lights are on, but nobody's home' kinda thing. And let's face it – we think a lot!

What's incredible, though, is that you will experience emotions whether you are present in an experience or just thinking about it. There is absolutely no difference in your sensory receptors. You will feel the emotions whether you like them or not.

So, ponder this for a minute: if you are constantly jumping from past files to the imaginary future and feeling your thoughts attached to either past files or imaginary future files, and you are hardly ever present in the present tense...

...then is your life really **REAL?**

Hmmmmm...

Fooled By The Biggest Illusion

What we need to realize is that we have been fooled by the biggest illusion this Universe has ever created.

We think we are experiencing reality, but what we are actually experiencing is our own thinking. The way our mind works is not like a camera that sees what's in the outside world, but rather like a projector of our own thoughts. We don't see a car – we see our thoughts about a car. We don't see people as they are – we see them as our thoughts or feelings about them. Whatever you think you are currently experiencing is just your own thoughts projected onto the screen of your own consciousness.

Whether you are experiencing something pleasant or awful right now will depend on what has been stored in your memory files from the past – as all those files come flooding in and project onto your conscious screen.

To explore this even further let me make a bold statement: your past doesn't even exist – except inside your own head. Nobody else has the same past as you. Sure, you have experienced a lot of things, some even had a terrible impact on your life – but were they real things or just your **interpretation** of events? You are not experiencing past events; you are experiencing your own thinking!

Anybody who has ever suffered from depression simply got their program stuck on 'repeat' – going over and over their own memory files of negative thoughts or feelings associated with something. Not only are the files being flashed back over and over again, but our 'Siri' is building up a bigger and bigger story around what you are 'seeing'. It's creating **meaning** out of the images. It's nothing to do with reality. It's like a CD stuck on repeat...it's not their situation that is depressing them; it's a glitch in the system that flashes those thoughts and feelings on repeat, ridiculously snowballing some attached horrendous meaning.

Unless this 'glitch' in the program is recognized as a programing fault and adjusted, those negative feelings and thoughts can compound over time and sometimes even lead to self-destruction. Gosh, what I would give to make people realize that there is nothing wrong with them – it's just their program that needs to be re-coded.

The same goes for the future. The future does not exist either – except for the thoughts that you are cooking up right now in your own head. You are running a program which is fetching files from the past and is predicting the future. Ever wondered how many of the things you worried about in the past actually happened? Your worrying and predictions are as accurate as trying to guess Lotto numbers.

Ever had an anxiety problem? Guess what? You were just making that stuff up! Literally! It's not that the feelings are not real – oh, yes, they are very, very real. They always are! Each thought as per its design comes with a feeling; they are inseparable. It's just that whatever you are worried about does not exist – except in your own head! You are literally stressing over a very realistic and painful-looking **mirage**!

Whoa! Now, that's enlightening!

If you can truly grasp this concept, your life will never be the same!

We think we live in a world of external experiences. Something happens out there in the world, and we believe we feel something in response. The direction of this process is what we get wrong. Even though it looks like the cause of our feelings is these external circumstances, this outside thing that's happening to us, in reality the true cause of our feelings in any given moment is actually our **own** thinking. It comes from **inside**, not outside!!!!

Take a deep breath now!

OK, are you ready to take this even further?

Have you ever been in a cinema watching an intense movie where you are **so** engrossed in the storyline that you jump off the seat when there is a sudden noise? That you cry or you laugh at certain points? We all know that a good movie is one that totally sucks us into a storyline. And one that has lots of unexpected twists and turns and keeps our emotions on a rollercoaster...

That experience would be even better if the movie were in 3D. Big difference, don't you think? So realistic!

Those of us who have been lucky enough to experience some crazy fun theme parks, like the Epcot Center for example, might have come across even more sophisticated movies: where they also have movement of the seats, the feel of raindrops, smells, and wind blowing in your hair. Suddenly that movie lifts the bar of the whole experience. It's so real!

What if you were upgraded to a virtual reality movie? Have you ever experienced one of those? Now, that's another step up in reality. Suddenly it feels like you are inside a movie. It feels so real: you reach out to grab onto stuff, you duck away from an oncoming object, you get dizzy or fall over from the motion... it feels so, so realistic!

Let's keep going. What if somebody just handed you a virtual reality suit called the 'body' and made you the main character in that virtual reality game? Wouldn't that feel **real**? As in SUPER real? As in...

Oh wait! Really?

What if your whole life was nothing more than a **VIRTUAL REALITY GAME**?

What if YOU were the main character in this virtual reality game? In your own virtual reality suit, called the body, which houses a colony of 37.2 trillion programmed cells (DNA).

What if you were directed by a self-learning program (subconscious mind) which learns from other virtual characters how to survive? You slowly develop your virtual personality, called the EGO, and get to experience 'LIFE' and feelings from that ego's perspective?

Holy shit! Is this possible?

Yep, it sure is! Just think about it. Even kids these days have computer games like The Sims, for example, where they can choose a character and play the role until the character dies. They can choose jobs, have kids, build homes...

This computer game was created by humans – is it so hard to believe that the Universe could create something like this in real life? A virtual game?

You bet!

Not only is it possible but, knowing what you know now, how can it not be? All you have to do is SLOW the heck down and look around you! Listen to all the conversations. How many people are you surrounded by that are not constantly jumping from past to future? Are they really beings living in the present or are they just in a trance-like state?

Most people are experiencing constant psychological drama. You can have 1,000 people in one room and everybody is in a different world – nobody is in reality! Lights are on but no-one is home. No-one is really **living** – everyone is just thinking about life and their dramas.

The psychological space has taken over the existential process of life. You do not experience life – you are only thinking about and reacting to situations around you. Thoughts and feelings are dominating everything. Your mind is either stuck in the past or predicting the future. Being present is a fleeting luxury...

Welcome to your own life, fondly referred to as **THE MATRIX!**

But, if this is the case, what can you do about it? Is there a way you can benefit from it? Yes, you sure can!

First and foremost, you need to awaken and realize that you are living in this illusion, which incidentally you have created on your own (with some help from your tribe, covered at the beginning of this book). Once you realize that you are creating your own 'reality', you can tune into the power of the Universal Mind and, with its help, literally redesign your whole life!

Just like at the movies, I sure hope that this book acts like a tap on the shoulder that can snap you to the reality that what you are watching on the screen is a projection of yourself caught up in your own world of thought. The minute you realize that, everything will become clear. You will forever drop the shackles of limitations and live life at a **totally** different level.

You can do this by first recognizing that your subconscious, conditioned mind is NOT YOU! The game itself makes you think you are the ego, the mask, the actual virtual reality character – but that's not true!

Most of us will go through life never ever realizing that – but, once **you** do, the game of life will just get so much sweeter!

From when you were born until now, you have been fooled by this illusion. Since the subconscious mind operates more than 95% of the time, it's easy to identify with the character and really think that you are it.

The best way to recognize when the program is overrunning you is to see what tense you are operating in. You as the real you, the Universal Mind, the creative energy, the co-master of your own universe, only operates in the present tense – NOW is all there is!

Ego, the fictional character your mind has created, constantly jumps from past to future; to it, the present moment doesn't exist.

The ego creates itself through the past – it's obsessed about it, going over and over past experiences, because without the past it doesn't really exist. It must have a reference point. So it creates different meanings about your experiences – meanings that align with all the beliefs already accepted – and then makes you revisit 'the past' over and over and over again so that you remember you are this character.

The ego also constantly projects itself onto the future, ensuring its continual survival. It makes you chase happiness in the future by saying, 'If I buy this, then I am going to be happy,' 'If I get this job, then I am going to be happy,' 'If I get a bigger house, then I am going to be happy,' 'If I become a famous YouTuber, I will be happy,' 'If I become rich, I will be happy.' And on and on and on it goes, therefore leaving you constantly unfulfilled and unsatisfied, and chasing this 'happiness mirage'.

Those of us who constantly set up future goals know that most of them will never really satisfy us when we achieve them – we will need to chase another goal. That's just the ego ensuring you have the carrot in front of you to further develop and sustain that particular character.

But, when you stop for a minute and bring your mind to the present tense, everything suddenly seems different. When you manage to snap yourself out of that movie you constantly play in your head, you no longer have to deal with depression, stresses or anxieties, as they do not exist in the present tense. Unless you are being physically hurt right now, there is nothing in the present tense that can cause you to feel stressed.

Even if you think you are going through something horrible right now, it's your 'life drama' created by your ego that is causing it. Stop for a second and think about this for yourself: what is your problem **right now**? No, I don't mean go over your files from the past or glimpse at what your ego is telling you about the potential future – I mean NOW!!

In the brilliant book 'The Power of Now', Eckhart Tolle explains that our ego constantly feeds on creating problems that it needs to 'solve'. It's also a master manipulator ensuring that it will never be found out because finding it would mean death to the ego.

Unfortunately, when the ego or mask engages you to identify with it, you constantly jump from past to future.

Problems mean that you are stressing over something mentally without there being any real intention or possibility of taking action now. You become so overwhelmed by your life drama that you lose your sense of life – of being. The bigger the problem your mind creates, the more it shows you that you need it. And so we go on to analyze the heck out of everything. The more intelligent and analytical you consider yourself to be, the more punishment you will receive in the form of problems to be solved – after all, that's the only way your ego will survive.

Most of the pain we create in our lives is totally unnecessary. Most of the pain you are creating is some sort of non-acceptance. Some type of judgment, or negativity. The intensity of the pain depends on how strongly you identify with your ego. The ego always seems to deny the now and escapes from it. The more you identify with your ego, the more you suffer.

The ego also needs to feel significant and self-important. It wants you to think it's super-smart, hence it will create disagreements with other egos. The funny thing is, when it comes to our smarts, the smartest thing we own is our smartphone in our pocket. All the ego knows is only the data it has collected over the years – a tiniest percentage of what there is to know. Even if you happen to have a whole library in your memory bank, you probably suck in comparison to your phone.

The ego, however, will fight for self-importance, therefore making you argue with other humans – and all that is is two egos not wanting to die. If you pay close attention during someone's argument, you will see that all their ego is doing is jumping from past to future, past to future – and recovering different data they have stored. Quite amusing, really!

The more you can accept the **now**, the more you are free from suffering. The ego cannot function without time, which is past and future. So it perceives the present tense as threatening. Time and ego are in fact inseparable. The ego even covers the present moment with the past or treats it as a means to get to something in the future. Watch out for that sneaky little parasite as it carries all the negative emotions!

If you manage to bring your consciousness to the present tense, your suffering suddenly stops. Interestingly, people who like dangerous sports get addicted to them because 'all their problems disappear' when they engage in such sports.

Say you love car racing. When such precision is required, the subconscious mind shuts down and gives space to the conscious Universal Mind because it **has** to be present as it can be a life or death situation. No time for daydreaming. That 'thrill' that these people get from the sport is not necessarily from the sport itself but is the thrill of the Universal Mind (through the receiver of our conscious mind) being in the flow and in total control – this is why it's so enjoyable and so addictive.

Anytime you will allow the Universal Mind to guide you, you are so much more powerful! All high-risk sports automatically pause the subconscious mind because it's too risky for the computer to handle it.

A lot of artists also refer to this state as 'being in the flow'. Have you ever done something where it was so enjoyable you totally lost sense of time? Yep, that's because in that moment your conscious Universal Mind was driving! And, as we've just learned, for the **real you** there is no such thing as time!

By realizing the game your ego plays, you will be able to snap yourself from that proverbial virtual reality game in the blink of an eye. It's like having the know-how to pull your mask off and see a whole bunch of people fighting and yelling at…thin air. The more enlightened you become, you'll have a greater edge in really experiencing the game of life. You just have to be present. Be in the NOW.

So, if you are a spirit in this proverbial virtual reality game of life, what's the purpose of it all? What's the meaning of life? How do you master this game?

I'm glad you asked!

How To Master The Game Of Life

What if the way to master the game of life is not to win wars and control others? What if it's not to become rich and buy half of the world? What if it's not to become a famous YouTuber? What if it's not to live your life in a way that does not disappoint your parents? What if it's not to be the best 'soldier' behind your mask?

What if the way to master this game was the AWAKENING?

Awakening to the fact that YOU ARE IN A 'VIRTUAL REALITY GAME'.

Awakening to the fact that you are surrounded by people who have been hijacked by their subconscious minds and whose egos are hiding the real them.

Awakening to the fact that you are stuck in 'The Matrix' of your own thinking.

The minute you realize that, you wake up! You self-actualize! You wake up to the possibility of having unlimited potential as you are connected to the actual Universal Mind. In fact, you are connected to every organism on Earth. Just like an ocean is represented by billions of waves – every one of them made up of the same thing: the ocean – you too are the energy that has divided itself into billions of particles; some into humans, some into animals and others into plants.

You are here in this 'game of life' to experience everything there is to experience. Just like you go to the movies to entertain yourself, life is a sophisticated game that entertains your soul.

And here is the most important thing: once you are aware of 'being in the game', you can tap into that Universal Mind that's a part of you and recreate your reality to one of your choosing and NOT the one you have been conditioned to.

Catch The Thief On Time

The most important thing is to catch yourself when your subconscious is taking over. Not all the time, of course – there is a reason why you had the computer installed in the first place. It's an amazing program which takes care of all your necessities, like any good 'General' should. But there are times where you need to be in charge and not hide behind your unconscious mind, otherwise known as your ego.

The good news is your feelings will help you navigate whether you are being manipulated by subconscious conditioning. Any time you feel depressed, overly sad or somehow grieving, realize that your EGO has taken you into your head and it's showing you a montage of something in the **past**. ON REPEAT!

Your ego is doing this so that you realize how 'helpless' you are without its protection. Any incident that you are replaying in your head over and over again, if analyzed, is simply a filtered confirmation of something that happened to you when you were a child, i.e. in the past.

It all boils down to two possible faults in your programing. Sometime in your childhood you have decided that you were either:

- Not good enough
- Not lovable enough

That's it. Whatever it is that is now stuck on repeat in your head is confirmation of either one or the other. The reason it's confirming this is NOT that any of this is true – it's just simply that the system, under its design, has to prove that you are 'right'. Remember, once a belief is accepted into your mind, even if you were only two at the time and it was randomly placed there by some adult who probably didn't even mean to, all you will be gathering now is confirmation of its being true.

How do you stop it? Simple! Any time you feel this feeling of sadness or stress, stop in your tracks and imagine yourself in a virtual reality (VR) game in your body suit. Look at your surroundings as if you were watching it in a game through your virtual reality eye mask. **Imagine taking your VR mask off**. Take a deep breath and find something nature created. A leaf, a flower...anything. Look at it. Look at its shape, texture, color...this will automatically bring you to the present tense.

Learning how to take that proverbial virtual reality mask off is the RESET BUTTON I was referring to in my introduction. It can be done in the blink of an eye and it is absolutely priceless. Please re-read the last paragraph and let it sink in – as in, really sink in! Your life will never be the same!

The ego, which was initially created by your mind like a protective older sibling, has now totally hijacked the real you. It's constantly proving that it's more important than you and that you need to stay under its 'protection'. Like a magician flicking through cards, it hypnotizes you. Like a thief on the street, it has its way of stealing from you. It's stealing from the potential of who you can become. The thing is, once you learn its tricks, it will never have the power over you again.

Now, I know I said it was **simple**. It's not **easy**, though. Your subconscious mind is super-powerful and has been playing tricks on you forever, so be patient with yourself.

Sure, it might fool you from time to time but, the more practice you put in, the quicker you will be able to recognize the trick.

Same goes for being anxious about something. Being anxious is just your mind's trick to drag you into the imagined future tense and create a 'monster situation' from which only the ego can protect you. Be careful with this. Things like procrastination, fear and perfectionism are the triggers, and should send you an alarm that it's that trickster ego trying to take over.

Are you procrastinating with something? That's your ego taking over.
Are you waiting for the perfect moment? That's your ego taking over.

The difference between a person who gets their mind under control and someone who doesn't is like seeing a K9 dog with its owner vs the barking uncontrolled mutt running from tree to tree. When a dog is trained to truly serve its owner, it turns into the most amazing friendship and companion. If left untrained, however, it will constantly be pulling you in all different directions, chasing cats, barking at random stuff and peeing on all the trees to show they like them (social media 'likes' anyone?). Which dog would you rather have in your life? One that serves you, checks in with you, pre-empts your needs and loves you unconditionally, or a spoiled brat that runs its own show?

Anyway, I think you get the picture...without proper training of your mind – and I am not talking university degrees here – the subconscious mind will forever be driving you around and you will be stuck in the 'passenger seat', watching your life go by.

It's time to get behind the wheel and be present to your own life.

The first step in your mind training is to constantly bring it back to the present tense. Whenever you feel something is off, or you have a negative feeling, imagine **being in the virtual reality game**. I really mean it. Just imagine yourself being inside your body in the body suit and everything around you is like a sophisticated computer game. Stop and look around at everything. Just stop. Breathe. Then imagine 'taking off your mask'. Look around. And I mean look at everything – at people around you, nature, objects. Look, listen and feel. It's all a game, just an illusion. A sophisticated, high-tech game. An incredible virtual game of life.

Most people can train their mind through meditation. Meditation is brilliant, and I highly recommend it. However, I find that a quick 'snap straight out of the virtual reality game' works much faster. It does take time to get used to the weirdness of the idea, but it's a brilliant strategy. Stop. Be present. Look at everything with wonder.

Now, imagine a huge light being switched on inside you, like a beam flowing into your body – that's your real energy. That's you. You are part of the infinite mind – your internet highway that knows all there is to know. That's the Universal Mind. Link into it. Be it. This is your factory setting – a loving, caring energy. You don't need to hide! You are awesome, you are lovable and you are sure as heck good enough to be here. Somebody **has** put you in this game after all! This is where you belong!

There are **no** barriers to what you can do. You can choose to be whatever you want. You are creative. You are here to experience life to the fullest degree. You don't need to find yourself. You are not here to fit into boxes, sit in the shadows or tiptoe through life to make it safely to death – oh, no! You are here to create and express yourself in any way you like. You are here to experience what life has to offer, to love, to care, and to create and connect. That is the real you, so don't let no ego hide you in the shadows. Let no ego fool you into believing you need to chase something to prove your worth. You don't need protection. You don't have to jump through any hoops to prove yourself. You are perfect just the way you are. You are whole.

You are a magnificent human being, and the more you hold onto that inside light, or energy, the more you will start noticing how life will start stacking up in your favor. You will suddenly start meeting people with 'lights on' and slowly you will progress into another life's dimension where everything around you is brighter, shinier and more alive.

If you have ever fallen in love you've probably already had experience in that dimension – in a split second **everything** is amazing. Food tastes better, colors are brighter, and there is music everywhere. Your senses are suddenly heightened, and you feel on top of the world. In a split second, all your problems disappear. That is the dimension of the game you belong in.

What most people don't know, however, is that this 'honeymoon' period can last a lifetime. I am not just talking about relationships; I am talking about your whole life. The only time that the honeymoon period is gone is when you let your subconscious take over. Incidentally, most relationships stop being in their honeymoon period as soon as their subconscious kicks in and tries to protect them from illusions of not being good enough – both partners put up a wall and there goes the honeymoon period.

OK, I'm Awake – Now What?!
Welcome To The Next Level Of Your Consciousness!

The process of the 'Great Escape' is described in detail in the following chapter, and if you follow it step by step you will be able to redesign your life to take you way beyond your current Matrix, the conditioning that you currently have.

If you follow it step by step, you will get amazing results. Ideally, it would be great if you could allow yourself some time off, preferably somewhere in nature with a journal where you can really concentrate on this process and take lots of notes.

I highly recommend you print out the journal I have created for you, which will act as a guide to this process. It is free of charge for my readers and will be extremely helpful in redesigning your new blueprint.

Go to www.quantummindacademy.com to download the journal free of charge. It is in a digital format and you can either type answers as you read it on your computer, or print it and use it as a hard-copy journal. Make sure you get it!

You will find the journal:
Under the section: BOOK
Your password is: CODING101
Once ready with journal in hand, put your creative hat on and let's create your best life ever!

PART 3
Preparation for the Great Escape

Most people never really put any conscious thought into what they really want. In fact, if you complete the exercises in the following chapters, you will be in the top 1% of people in the world who know what they want.

Most people just assume that they must go with the flow and deal with everyday life as it comes. Now that you understand how the mind actually works and how the three principles of the Universal Mind, Consciousness and Thought have created this incredible illusion, this is the time to ask yourself the question: what do I really want?

Before you answer the question, please understand that life is about creation and expression of your soul – it is **not** about competition with other souls. We are all here to create something incredible, progress evolution and experience life in human form.

For those who have woken up from the computerized state and progressed to the 'next level' of consciousness, life is ABUNDANT! Yes, you can have it all – all you have to do is define what your version of 'abundance' looks like...

Find Your Groove

Most people go through life not really knowing what they want. It's not something we are taught how to do. Let's face it, with all the conditioning we have received as children, most of us have just moved along the path of life without much intention.

In fact, if life were a river, a lot of us have spent it either struggling against the current or screaming our lungs out going down a massive waterfall of unfortunate events, crashing against branches and rocks along the way.

But what if life could be simpler? What if you could find your own groove and move with ease to exactly where you are meant to go, occasionally gracefully navigating around some rocks and pebbles along the way?

In order to be able to do that, you need to first figure out where it is you were meant to go.

Every plant on Earth has inside it a seed with its entire DNA coding, which tells them what they will become. An acorn is not meant to become a palm tree, just like a palm seed doesn't wish to become an oak tree. Sure, you can try some genetic modification, but ideally you would love to let nature take its course and let it grow to what it was meant to be.

You are no different. You have a 'seed' inside you, excited to get planted and, given the right environment to grow, thrive and become what you were meant to become. It's important to figure out what type of seed it is so that you can provide it with the best environment to grow. There's no point to planting ferns in Antarctica!

Now, don't panic yet – it's not that hard to figure it out. Deep, deep down you already know what it is. You have an internal GPS system which can guide you – you just have to learn to listen to it. It's called intuition.

One of the biggest problems that interfere with your intuition channel is your ego trying to play the role it has created. Egos forever try to either win the game, be more significant, fit in or please others. The ego overanalyzes stuff according to its conditioning.

It's grossly influenced by what success 'should look like' according to media or peers. It's chasing goals like some Pokémon*, ticking them off because others have done them. It's also distracted by short-term pleasures which might or might not be that good for your soul.

Just like the analogy we used earlier, if a seedling is told to be something else in order to be successful, there will always be an internal conflict – and that is what the influence of media, social media and people around you can do to you. The world around you is loud and, the quicker you find the temporary mute button, the better.

The only way to tune into your intuition, which is whispering inside you, is to slow down, quiet the noise around you, ask the right question and listen for an answer.

---

*Pokémon are virtual characters in a cell phone game that projects a character onto a real street. It was originally developed in Japan to promote physical activity and by 2019 had over a billion users worldwide. People ran down streets to find their Pokémon, which gave them points. It got so ridiculous that all you saw were people walking down the streets, constantly looking at their phones to locate their Pokémon. Many governments eventually banned the game because there were too many accidents: some players were hit by cars, others fell off cliffs. All in the name of a game.

Many, many super-successful people around the world take some time out to actively listen to their intuitions. Some do it every day through morning meditation, a walk in nature, swimming, taking baths, or just sitting still and observing nature. Literally anything that allows you to be present with nature without any distractions will do the trick.

Taking this a step further, successful people also often schedule a few days out every year, some more often, to slow down and have their 'compass adjustment time'. No distractions, no phones, no televisions – just nature and you. That is by far the best way of tuning into the real you as sometimes it takes a day or two to slow down your crazy-busy mind…

Shortly I will ask you a few questions which might help you with tuning into the right channel of your intuition and figuring things out for yourself. These questions can be found in the journal you can download for free from my website www.quantummindacademy.com. Allow yourself some 'me time' to answer them. Ideally, you will want to do this with pen and paper, and somewhere in nature where you cannot be disturbed. Leave your cell phone behind.

Let's figure out what your 'passion' is as this is the path that we will follow. But, before we do, let me just clarify and simplify something for you.

There is so much hype in the world about following your passion.

In fact, it's so drummed into us that people sometimes get freaked out because they don't know what their passion is and where the heck to find it. We are told to follow it, to peruse it, to flow with it – but how on earth do you do that if you have no idea what it is you are looking for?

Passion would have to be one of the biggest misconceptions in the world. It's not a treasure hunt where if you look hard enough you will find it. It's not in your ideal next partner, it's not in your dream job, it's not on the next mountain you climb. In fact, it's not **anything tangible** you can find! And it sure as heck does not reside **outside** of you!

Passion is what you GIVE!

Passion is the energy that you put into something you like **doing**. Passion is something that you feel inside, the higher vibration of fun and joy and love.

It's the energy that pours **out** of you – and the more energy you give the more it makes you feel like you are 'high' on life.

You know when you sometimes flick through different radio channels and your favorite song comes on…yessss, the bliss! You just feel it. It absolutely resonates with you. And you could listen to it over and over again. There is a vibration in it that just makes you feel lighter. And happier. And moves you. That's the energy I am talking about.

What are some activities that you do that make you totally forget the time?

_____
_____
_____

What is it about that activity that you enjoy most?

_____
_____
_____

What would you do even if you were doing it for free?

_____
_____
_____

What activity energizes you?

_____
_____
_____

What are you curious about?

_____

_____

_____

What brings you joy?

_____

_____

_____

_____

Now, this is a slightly harder question:
If you were to look at your life thus far, what were your peaks and your lows?

_____

_____

_____

_____

_____

What we don't realize is that our internal GPS is constantly guiding us. It's selecting experiences for us which will help us grow in the direction we are meant to go in. Sometimes those experiences can be very, very painful, but it's the person we become on the other side of this experience that can achieve the greater good – like a seedling that pushes past massive rocks in search of the sun.

The experiences that we have experienced in the past have not happened **to** us but **for** us. Each problem we have encountered was there to make us grow and evolve as human beings. It's that growth that made us strong. It's that growth that can be harnessed into something incredible.

In a Stanford commencement speech Steve Jobs once said:

'You can't connect the dots looking forward; you can only connect them looking backwards. So you have to trust that the dots will somehow connect in your future. You have to trust in something – your gut, destiny, life, karma, whatever. This approach has never let me down, and it has made all the difference in my life.'

With the help of this book you can learn to recognize the dots ahead of you much more quickly – like the markers on a trail.

With that in mind, let's analyze your 'past dots' a little more and see where they have been pointing you thus far.

What were the five hardest/most challenging experiences of your life?

1.
2.
3.
4.
5.

If you were to describe positive growths you have received from them, what would they be?

1.
2.
3.
4.
5.

What were the most triumphant/joyful experiences of your life?

1.
2.
3.
4.
5.

Was there an extremely challenging/terrible experience that you went through in your life that made you stronger? It should be an experience that you wouldn't want anyone to ever go through.

_____

_____

_____

_____

What were the most important lessons you learned from it?

_____

_____

_____

_____

Knowing what you know now, **whom** could you help with this knowledge?

_____

_____

_____

_____

What have you learned from it which can help others avoid it?

_____

_____

_____

_____

_____

Whom would you like to help?

_____

_____

_____

_____

_____

Are you starting to see a pattern?

Now that we have put some of our past dots into focus and we have established some kind of pattern, let's see how those dots might pan out in the future. Just remember, as a co-writer of your own story/virtual reality game, you want to follow your feelings of fulfillment. There is no need to be precise with your plan as the Universe has a certain way of always surprising you.

Below are three scenarios with even more questions which are thought provoking and might be of great help.

Visualize yourself being 90 years old, sitting in your rocking chair with a bunch of kids around you. Maybe they are your great-grandkids; maybe they are just some neighbors' rascals. They sit around you on the floor having a conversation with you. Just imagine them being curious about you. They ask you to tell them about your life.

What stories will you tell them?

_____
_____
_____
_____
_____

What have you achieved?
(Concentrate on the years between **now** and 90 years old)

_____
_____
_____
_____
_____

Now try this question:

It's your 80th birthday. You are at your own birthday party. Your friends are coming up one by one to a microphone and telling anecdotes about your life. What are they saying?

_____

_____

_____

_____

They also seem to be very thankful. What are they thanking you about?

_____

_____

_____

_____

_____

_____

_____

Answering the above questions will get you thinking about what's really important in your life. They say that nobody on their deathbed says, 'I wish I spent more time at the office' – rather, they all talk about friendships, love and little things that mattered. What were those things for you? The more specific you can be with your answers, the clearer your vision will become.

The quickest way to work out what's **important** to you is to imagine you were just told you had six months to live. What would you do? The answer to this question will get straight to the core of what's important to you.

_____

_____

_____

_____

_____

Now that you have a better vision for your future life, let's write a kick-butt blueprint for your new life.

Create A Blueprint – The Game Changer

Before you get stuck into writing another goal list or, worse, to-do list, understand that to be really clear about what you want is not as simple as just writing a bunch of goals – you know, the ones you do every January 1st. A lot of those items are simply stuff that you think you might want based on your current beliefs and influences from media – you know, bigger house than Bob's or better Bahamas trip to compete with Mary or more chiseled abs than Jonathan.

Instead, ask yourself the question: WHY?

Have you ever asked yourself why on earth do you want that Porsche or that career? There is nothing wrong with having those goals, by the way, but it's **super important** to ask yourself **WHY** you want them.

'So that' goals are the ones that society tells us we need to have to achieve happiness. It's getting a certain degree, being with a certain someone, reaching a certain income. They are the 'Pokémon' we think we need to collect to win the game – get into such-and-such school **so that** you can get a certain job, **so that** you can get a certain income, **so that** you can get promoted, **so that** you can get more money, **so that** you can buy this house, **so that** you can get this girl, **so that** you can buy this car, **so that** people can be envious, **so that** you are respected, **so that** you can make your parents proud, **so that** you feel loved.

Every time you write a goal ask yourself: **why**? Why do I really want it? What is my **final** goal?

The more you ask yourself the question WHY, the quicker you will realize that you are chasing a certain feeling that the achievement of the goal will give you, **not** the actual goal.

You don't really want a Lamborghini per se – you just want the **feeling** it will give you when you drive it, whether it's the speed and adventure you are after or the feeling of admiration from your peers, envy from your colleagues, feeling of significance, or 'love' from the opposite sex.

Interesting! Make sure you get to the bottom of it. You don't want to waste most of your life chasing some mirage just to realize that what you were craving is something much, much simpler and can be achieved without the headaches attached.

I remember years ago I dreamed about owning a health retreat. I had visions of exactly what it would look like, what treatments it would provide and what the accommodation would be. I was quite excited about this massive goal of mine and I would tell anybody who would listen. What can I say, I was an ambitious 19 year old.

One day I flew up to one of those fancy retreats for a week to see how they operated. I loved it, of course, **but** while sunbathing by the pool I noticed something interesting. I overheard one of the employees talking to another about one of the beauty therapists calling in sick. Suddenly everybody was running around in control damage because the treatments were scheduled back to back and, as we were located in a very remote area, replacing that employee was not an option. It was hard watching them stress out, reshuffling the appointments and being told off by entitled patrons about why their service was not good enough. As this scene unfolded in front of me, I remember sipping on my orange juice while dangling my feet in the water and asking myself: **why** the heck do I want to **own** a health retreat?

The answer came back at me immediately: because you want to feel important, be healthy, meet like-minded people, make them feel good and use a retreat whenever you feel like it - for free!

WOW!!! I certainly wasn't expecting this answer to be so blunt! But what it made me realize is that I could achieve my goal of 'feeling significant, being healthy, finding like-minded people, making them feel good and going to retreats' without investing millions of dollars in owning a retreat, with all its glory **and** headaches attached. In fact, I could join a group of 'health junkies' and travel around the world sampling different retreats without even once worrying about staffing issues. All I had to do was increase my income slightly to cover the expense.

See, what we sometimes do not think about is that with every goal comes new responsibilities and struggles. We all want to look amazing, but not all of us are willing to give up those chocolates, cheeses and 5 o'clock drinks. We all want to be rich, but not many of us are willing to pull our sleeves up and put in the hours and sweat required. We all want to attract an amazing partner but some are not willing to go through the deep conversations, vulnerability and giving of love, which allows us to keep them.

When choosing your goals it's important to analyze them so that we know they will lead to long-term happiness. Not only do we need to look at the benefits but we also need to identify the sacrifices it will take to achieve them. If it's the sacrifices and the struggles (i.e. growth) that excite you – then you're onto a winner. But, if you are only chasing a goal without looking at the downside, you are in for a shocking surprise.

Here is a little, well-known anecdote which explains this concept a little more:

The parable of a Fisherman and an Investment Banker as told in 'The 4-Hour Work Week'

It goes like this…

'An American investment banker was at the pier of a small coastal Mexican village when a small boat with just one fisherman docked. Inside the small boat were several large yellowfin tuna. The American complimented the Mexican on the quality of his fish and asked how long it took to catch them.

The Mexican replied, "Only a little while."

The American then asked why didn't he stay out longer and catch more fish.
The Mexican said he had enough to support his family's immediate needs.

The American then asked, "But what do you do with the rest of your time?"

The Mexican fisherman said, "I sleep late, fish a little, play with my children, take siestas with my wife, Maria, stroll into the village each evening where I sip wine, and play guitar with my amigos. I have a full and busy life."

The American scoffed, "I am a Harvard MBA and could help you. You should spend more time fishing and with the proceeds buy a bigger boat. With the proceeds from the bigger boat you could buy several boats; eventually you would have a fleet of fishing boats. Instead of selling your catch to a middleman you would sell directly to the processor, eventually opening your own cannery. You would control the product, processing, and distribution. You would need to leave this small coastal fishing village and move to Mexico City, then LA and eventually New York City, where you will run your expanding enterprise."

The Mexican fisherman asked, "But how long will this all take?"

To which the American replied, "15 – 20 years."

"But what then?" asked the Mexican.

The American laughed and said, "That's the best part. When the time is right you would announce an IPO and sell your company stock to the public and become very rich, you would make millions!"

"Millions – then what?"

The American said, "Then you would retire. Move to a small coastal fishing village where you would sleep late, fish a little, play with your kids, take siestas with your wife, stroll to the village in the evenings where you could sip wine and play your guitar with your amigos.'"

Once we ask ourselves enough whys, we will know if a goal is a 'so that' goal or is what we truly desire. It's like eating a coconut – you have to peel all the layers off before you get to the juicy part of what you really, really want.

If you ask enough whys you will find that the real goals are to do with joy, growth, love and contribution. These are the only things that your soul really craves. They are not the temporary dopamine hits, quick scores and 'likes' on your Instagram – they are much, much deeper than that.

Final goals speak to your soul. They are not the destinations you arrive at or Pokémon (stuff) you collect – they are the journeys you will embark on.

You are after **experiences** that you will remember for a lifetime – the experiences you will so fondly remember and talk about with those imaginary children from a previous chapter.

After all, it's not achievement of those goals that will bring happiness to your life. It's the growth and the progress and the person you will become along the way – **that** is what will make your life fulfilling.

The point of writing a blueprint is having that 'North Star' on your compass and knowing what you want but also allowing enough space for the Universe to surprise you with how it is achieved.

It's important to concentrate on the feelings you would like to feel and most importantly **why** you would like to feel them, and let the HOW be delivered by the Universe. Just trust that your Universal Mind has an amazing ability to deliver what you wish for but in 99% of cases it's in a way which you will not expect – sometimes in the most surprising way!

What if you could divorce yourself from the 'old story' of who you are and take on a new role – one that is intentional, custom made and consciously chosen by you?

In the next chapter you will find different categories of your life we need to put under the microscope. What experiences and feelings would make your 'cup' full of joy in each of these categories? Describe experiences you would like to experience.

Make sure, when you write, write in the present tense and include all your senses: what you see, what you hear, what you feel, what it smells like and what it tastes like (if applicable).

Your subconscious mind is a program, a program, which responds to visual stimuli. I will explain this a little more as we go through each category.

So here are your categories – in no particular order, all as important as each other. By having a deep dive into each one of these categories you will be able to assess what your limiting beliefs have been and replace them with beliefs that will allow you to achieve greatness in life.

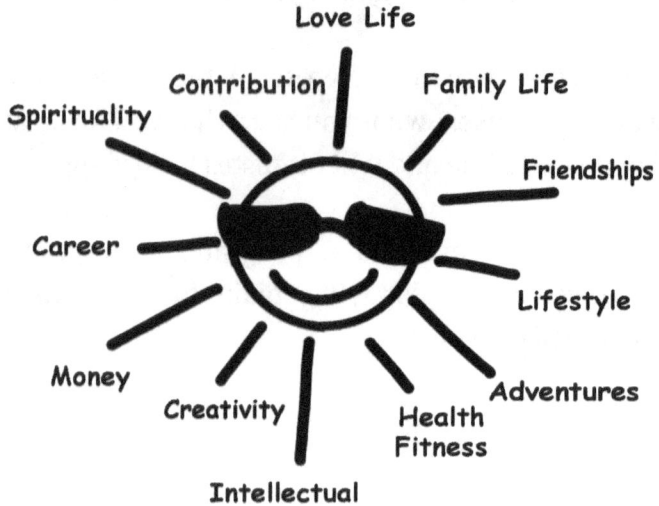

Love Life:

Love relationship is probably one of the most important relationships you will create as it can have a huge impact on all other categories of your life. Whether you are currently married, choose to be married in the future, be in a same-sex relationship or just have a love partner, it makes no difference. However, your choice of person will make an enormous impact on you and your life.

This is why I will spend a little more time on this category. Understand, however, that all your categories are just as important as each other. When you are designing your blueprint make sure you give them all as much time and attention as you give this one.

There are many 'ingredients' that constitute a great relationship, but four of them are like the pillars – the legs to a table; they will either hold up a great relationship or cause it to tumble down.

The four 'ingredients' are:

Consciousness – being aware that inside 'your' human there is a sensitive soul which needs to be seen, heard, loved, validated and respected. There is still that 'child' that needs to be loved. It doesn't matter how tough an adult's exterior gets, there is a softness and gentleness of the soul in everyone. You just need to be able to see it. Usually the tougher the exterior the harder that person had to fight to be loved. Being able to strip beyond the subconscious conditioning and connect to that soul will make the relationship soar to the next level.

The minute you become disconnected from that soul, 'love' turns into need, dependency and control. This is why love based on just lust without a stronger soul connection will never work, however attractive and exciting it might seem at first. Like a drug, it will give you a quick dopamine hit but then it will drain you, leaving you dependent and unsatisfied.

What's the difference between lust and love, you ask?
Let me give you a metaphor:

Seeing beautiful flowers, picking them and putting them in a vase – that's lust.
Seeing beautiful flowers, adding extra nutrients and watering them – that's love.

One is taking what you want; the other is giving your partner what they need.

Another way of looking at it is: a relationship without a 'soul connection' and love is sort of like having a computer without a Wi-Fi connection. Sure, it works for the basics, but there is so much more that you can have and be when the connection is there. Make sure you consciously seek out connection. Always. During all discussions, especially if arguments arise, ask yourself: 'Am I seeking control or am I seeking connection?' Whenever you find yourself seeking power and control, you can bet your bottom dollar your ego and subconscious mind are running the show and heading straight for the exit. Always seek understanding and connection, and your relationship will thrive.

Communication – being aware that both your mind and your partner's mind operate on cruise-control 95% of the time, you are responding to everything via program and not consciously.

The dating world might fool you into believing that in order to succeed you must be a better 'poker player' than your partner. Hence, we hold things back, play our best cards, tease, create tension, withhold communication and play games...

If you want a great relationship, you need to think of your partnership as a team game. Let's use basketball as an example – although you can use any other team sport if you prefer as they all work on the same principle. The reason the sport is so successful is that all players, referees and all the fans **know** and **understand** the **rules** of the game.

Just imagine if a couple of players got together occasionally to shoot some hoops – sure, it'll be fun. Then one day they decide to play a serious game, with referees, an audience and a television crew. They have been given referees who all have their own ideas of what is allowed and what is not allowed in the game. The players start playing but every few minutes they get pulled up by a referee for breaking a rule they didn't know about. They get told off. As they move to shoot a hoop, they get stopped again and told it should be done differently. Then they start having an argument with each other about which position on the court they should play. The game starts again, only to shortly be stopped by a yelling fan whose idea of the game is different. He tells the players what to do. The game starts. Then stops. And then starts again...

Let me ask you this: how long would you stay in that game even if you **really** liked shooting hoops? This is pretty much how most relationships unfold. You get together, have some fun and, before you know it, you are treading on ice trying to navigate someone else's minefields of uncommunicated expectations, dos and don'ts. You are trying to guess what the other person is thinking based on your own conditioning, but you seem to be breaking rules you didn't even know existed. Sooner or later, you get frustrated and you default to either not participating as much or just playing your own game. Both result in depletion of excitement and energy. The game is no longer fun.

Now, compare this to the comradery of a proper team – a basketball team, for example. The only reason it works well is that the players, the referees and the crowd watching know the **rules**! When you have clear boundaries of what's expected, what's not allowed and what makes the game exciting, the game becomes thrilling! As a player you can absolutely excel, become the best version of yourself and create an incredible connection with your teammates. The kind of tension or teasing in this kind of environment is never offensive – just super fun. You celebrate your wins and you learn from your losses. Together. You thrive and so does your partner! You both grow and develop into better players. It gets really, really exciting!

People love to watch you play – they are in awe! You and your teammate become unstoppable! Your absolute best!

This is the difference between a failed relationship and a thriving relationship. For a love relationship to be super-successful, it needs to have boundaries and rules – just like any exciting game would. Without these, it'll just be hit and miss, and sooner or later you will get bored. Or hurt. That's the bad news. The good news, however, is that you and your partner can **collaborate** on creating those rules. You both decide what it takes to make your relationship thrilling. What constitutes a 'win' and what is a no-go zone. The more you learn to communicate, the better the relationship can be. Just think of custom designing your best game ever – one you would want to play for a very, very long time! Even make it into a fun exercise and say to each other: if this were the relationship of your wildest dreams, what would it look like? Compare your notes and create a perfect game plan. In fact, design it in a way that you would never want it to end!

Vulnerability – great communication can be achieved only if you are willing to be vulnerable. Many mistake being vulnerable as opening themselves up to being attacked. That's not true, though – vulnerability is a massive strength in a relationship. Allowing your guard down is the only way to build true intimacy and connection with your partner. Being vulnerable in a relationship means allowing your partner to know you fully: your thoughts, feelings, challenges, weaknesses and desires. Without having this knowledge, you and your partner will not be able to create an incredible love relationship. Just like in a great sporting team, you need to know what your teammate's strengths and weaknesses are so that you can work better together.

Many experiments have been done in sport where they cherry-pick top players from different teams and create a 'team of champions' to play a game against another 'normal' great team. The expectations on the 'team of champions' were huge as, after all, they were the world's best of the best. To everybody's amazement, the 'team of champions' lost to the other team. Why? Because every player had an image to uphold and wanted to be the hero. It was all about them individually and **not** about the team they were playing in. There was no vulnerability. Just a whole bunch of 'heroes'.

This is why a well-rounded *champion team*, with all their strengths and weaknesses, will always be stronger than the *team of champions* (who are just in it for themselves). Every sports coach will tell you that!

Love relationships are no different. You just need to be willing to learn the ins and outs of how your partner 'plays', and that requires open communication and vulnerability.

We associate vulnerability with emotions we want to avoid, such as fear, shame and uncertainty. Yet we lose sight of the fact that it's also a birthplace of joy, belonging, creativity, authenticity and love – which are all needed to live a meaningful life and have incredible friendships and love relationships. After all, we all want to feel totally loved and totally accepted by someone.

Always remember that the goal of vulnerable disclosure is not resolution but connection.

For those of you who have trouble with opening up, I highly recommend reading 'The Power of Vulnerability' by Brené Brown.

Action – a lot of people think love is what you receive from someone but, again, this is not true. Love is not receiving – it is giving. Because the way we see others is actually the way we see ourselves, by withholding love from someone we withhold love from ourselves. You need to open yourself up to receiving love, and the only way to do it is by giving love.

In nature, either things grow or they die; there is no static. This is why love requires constant action. In order to have an extraordinary relationship you need two extraordinary people who can choose themselves on a daily basis, and that translates to constant growth and action.

A fascinating book called 'The 5 Love Languages' talks about how everyone communicates love in different ways, so understanding each other's specific love language may be beneficial to your relationship. According to Gary Chapman, Ph.D., the author of the book, once you and your partner have identified with one of the five languages, you will both feel most loved when that language is expressed and gain the satisfaction of making each other happy.

The five languages are (everybody has a different choice):

1. Quality time
2. Acts of service
3. Words of affirmation
4. Receiving gifts
5. Physical touch

By knowing which 'language' your partner prefers, you can work out how to best take action to show your love – not much point investing in expensive Gucci bags if your partner just needs quality time or you to tell them how much you admire their strength. Communication, communication, communication.

Gary Chapman has also created a really cool app called 'Love Nudge'. The app allows you to take a quiz and within minutes it will tell you and/or your partner what your preferred love language is. It also reminds you about little 'acts' you can do for your partner to make them feel loved. Yep, there is an app for everything!

It's so easy to become complacent in relationships, especially if your subconscious takes over. But always remember that a relationship is like a plant – if you forget to water it, however often it needs to be watered, it will eventually die!

Find out what your and your partner's love language is (i.e. what type of water you should feed it) and always remember to give your relationship plenty – even if it means being reminded by an app!

Now, let's get back to your blueprint. Take out your journal and write a few paragraphs about your ideal relationship. Whether you are in a relationship or not, it's helpful to know what you truly desire. What sorts of feelings would you like to experience on a continual basis? What is your love language, and how would you like your love to be shown? What character traits does your partner have? If you don't have a partner, what characteristics are you looking for? What sorts of things do you do? Describe everything in detail. Remember, the more detail you can add, the clearer your picture and the easier it will be for your subconscious mind to filter through seven billion people.

By the way, don't be a douchebag and concentrate on just the exterior. So many people date show ponies to try to boost their egos, only to find that they quickly get bored with the lack of depth in their personalities. Concentrate, rather, on what **values** are you looking for? What interests does the person have? What experiences do you share together? What does your average day together look like? Make sure you use the PRESENT TENSE.

Family Life:

Let's face it, not all your family members will support you on this journey, and that is OK. It is your job to recognize where everyone is at and treat them accordingly. You cannot rush someone's personal growth.

In your blueprint describe your ideal family life. This should include not just a spouse and children, if applicable, but also parents, siblings and anyone in your tribe you would like to spend more time with.

My own blueprint goes in depth into each one of my relationships with family members. How would I like to show up for each one of them? How often would I like to see them?

Describe your best average day. What do you celebrate? What experiences do you have with them? What is important to you in your family?

Friendships:

It's not what we have in life but who we have in our life that matters.

Friendships are extremely important to your wellbeing. Choose wisely!

Nurture friendships that inspire you. Get rid of the anchors in your life. Those who drain your energy (the energy vampires, as I call them) should not have your attention. Let them go.

And, if you cannot let them go, make it your mission to spend less time with them. Don't get involved in their dramas.

Your time on this Earth is very short – surround yourself with people who increase your energy, inspire you and support your growth.

Who are the people in your life who support your dreams?

Get crystal clear on your social values and attributes you would like your friends to have.

What are you looking for in your friends? Kindness? Responsibility?

What are the deal breakers? Dishonesty?

How would you like to spend time with your friends?

What experiences would you like to have together?

What do you celebrate?

What other friends would you like to attract into your life? What sorts of things do they like? How do you spend your time together?

Again, when you write, write in present time as if you are already living this life.

Adventures:

Don't ever underestimate how important are adventures in your life! It is the experiences of your life that you will be looking back on and smiling at – not stuff that you owned.

Adventures help you grow as a person because they challenge you to get out of your comfort zone. They give you a sense of accomplishment. They help you feel gratitude and mindfulness by keeping your conscious mind in the present tense. They often expand your horizons and your point of view, and teach you creative problem solving. Adventures allow you to meet new people, see different perspectives and become more open-minded. Unlike the stuff we buy that is meaningless in no time, travels, adventures and unusual experiences you will cherish and re-live forever.

Write a list of adventures you would like to embark on. What would they look like? Where would you go? Whom would you meet? What would you experience?

Lifestyle:

Describe in detail what would be your ideal lifestyle. What does your home look like? Your car? Your surroundings? Again, tap into that authentic self – this is not an Instagram quest to compete with others. What do you truly desire? Describe your perfect home environment. The more detail you can include, the better.

When you travel, what environment do you stay in? How do you travel? Do you stay at a resort, a boutique hotel, an Airbnb, a campsite? What does your environment look like?

The more you can visualize it, the better. I often like to go on a Google image search (or Pinterest) and come up with some images which could represent my lifestyle. Have fun with this one!

Health and Fitness:

We all know that without health you have nothing. Arguably, this should be your priority. You want to stay healthy and fit to truly enjoy this amazing blueprint of yours. If you are fit, your love life will definitely benefit. You will have more energy for your family and friends. You will have more energy to give it your best at your career and you will be more likely to have better adventures. Everything links back to good health.

Think of your body as a vehicle that needs to carry your soul through this journey of life. How do you treat it?

Describe in detail what your body looks like, from head to toe. My health and fitness description is two pages long and includes not just the external looks but the health of internal organs as well.

Most people just concentrate on the external but, if you think about it, there are 37.2 trillion cells operating inside your body – let them be fully nourished, oxygenated and clean.

What do you look like? How do you feel? What are the comments you are hearing from people around you? How do they make you feel?

Intellectual Life:

Your mind loves to grow. In fact, progress often equals happiness. What are some things you would love to learn? What are some things you would like to intellectually achieve? Writing this book was under my intellectual category, hence you are reading it right now. What sorts of things would get your mind excited? What skills would you like to develop?

Creative Life:

Creative life is essential for the soul. This is how your soul plays. If you can combine creativity with work, great, but it's not essential. Think of creativity as a child. You have two children: one is the brainy one, the other creative – they both need to be fed. If you feed only one, the other one will die. Make sure you give them both the attention they deserve. Choose an activity which you enjoy. Your soul will thank you for it. Oh, and also, don't put pressure on yourself to make a living out of your creative output. If it happens, great, but do it because you love it.

What creative activities do you like?
What could you do to explore your creativity further?
Are there any classes you could take?
Could you join a club?

Money:

To live the life you truly desire, what sort of income would you require? Remember, we need to be specific here. Don't just say 'a lot'. That is equivalent to going to a bank and asking a lady behind the counter to withdraw 'a lot' from your account – the person behind the desk will just give you a puzzled look. As you know, everybody's reality is different. Have a look at the lifestyle you would like to live. How much money annually would you require to fulfill this? Be as specific as you can, keeping in mind that your goals are now your goals. You don't need to keep up with the Kardashians of this world.

Come up with a figure that is specific to you.

Career:

A lot of people, especially those contemplating changing their career, get stuck on this question: what career should you work in? A great way to define it for your subconscious mind is to list all the things you would like your work to let you experience. Do you want to be challenged? And, if so, in what way?

Always remember that your work is not about your work – rather, your work is your greatest vehicle for your personal evolution. It helps you evolve to being a better human being.

What type of people would you like to work with? Do you travel or work from home? If you were to define your best working conditions, what would they look like? Don't be specific with career choice – let the career find you. When you open yourself up to possibilities, a surprising door might just open – something you haven't even contemplated. Remember, don't tell the Universe how to deliver your career; just give it a list of essentials. Go ahead and list 20 requirements.

Me Time/Spirituality:

Having space for your own time is very important – time to reflect, time to plan, time to meditate, time to re-code, time to just chill. In your ideal life how much 'me time' would you want to have and what sorts of things would you do? This category encompasses not only your spirituality but also your emotions. What sorts of feelings would you like to experience on a continual basis? What would make your soul sing?

Contribution:

One of my favorite Anthony Robbins quotes is:
'The reason for living is giving.'

It's through contribution that you build amazing relationships and intense fulfillment. This is your soul's real playground. Whether it's contributing your time, your skills or your money, everything counts. Remember, real love is GIVING, and there is no better way of experiencing love than through compassion and contribution. What sorts of skills do you have which could make a difference to another human being? Or to an animal? How would you like to contribute to this world?

Now that you understand you are a Spirit conveniently packaged up in a 'body suit', how would you like to contribute to your fellow souls? Remember that for your spirit to thrive you need only three things: love, growth and contribution. In which direction will you expand in those three areas?

If you would like to further develop your blueprint, I highly recommend my online course 'Life can be a dream', which will not only walk you through each category but make you dive deeper into all your limited beliefs you have had installed – replacing them with new ones, creating a brilliant vision and creating strategies to plug into your current life right now.

You can find more tools on our website at www.quantummindacademy.com.

Create Your Avatar

'We don't do what we can; we do what we are.'
Anthony Robbins

As children we were sometimes told that we could be whatever we wanted to be when we grew up...but then somehow a condition snuck in 'as long as it's in line with...' The rules of the tribe kicked in and you could become 'whatever you wanted' as long as you made them proud.

But what if this were true? What if you indeed could be anything you wanted to be? Without any conditions? What if you had a chance to sit down with your 'screenwriter' and rewrite your whole character of the person you are playing right now?

The reason you haven't yet achieved some of the things you have included in your new blueprint is that your ego was not aligned with your new mission. This is why it is crucial to create a new character to take over from the current ego. We are going to call it your Avatar. In the gaming world, 'avatar' is a word used for a fictional character we choose to become. Your Avatar will be a mix of your current character (keep only the positive attributes) and lots of new additional upgrades.

The quickest way to change your life is not through wishes and wants and controlling of negative thoughts and behaviors – it's through an actual **identity shift**.

It's like in the movies: different actors are suited to different roles. You would never have Bart Simpson play the role of Superman – unless it were a comedy. It's the same in your life:

your character needs a bit of an upgrade to be able to execute your blueprint.

So what exactly is an 'identity shift'? Think about it this way. There is a difference between someone who tries not to drink too much alcohol and an **abstinent**. A person who chooses to eat less meat and a **vegetarian**. A person who exercises and an **athlete**. One is to do with what you prefer and the other is to do with whom you are! One is a choice (which is based on how you feel at the time), the other one is an IDENTITY. One is persuadable, the other one is respected!

If you are a person who needs a healthier lifestyle, pushing yourself into exercising and dieting because you 'have to' or 'should' will last only as long as your strong will sustains it. The minute, however, you take on an **identity** of either an 'athlete' or a 'fitness goddess', you no longer have to push yourself to eat healthily or move as it's an absolute 'given' for these characters. This is who they are. An athlete does not have to force himself/herself to do anything – it's their true nature to eat healthily, avoid sugar, move their body and be energized. It's their **identity**. And, surprisingly, it can be **your** new identity if you so choose.

You can create an identity (your Avatar) which is an ideal self, and through simple re-coding of the subconscious you can literally step into that role and shift the whole reality of your Universe.

See, any actor who plays an incredible performance in any of your favorite movies will tell you that learning the lines is not enough – you must truly become the character you are playing. Actors become obsessed with learning everything there is to learn about their character – about who they are in their core.

They encompass all the emotions and then, just like that, they step into that role.

Your identity determines your beliefs. Your beliefs determine your behavior.

Therefore, your **identity shapes your everyday choices** – and this is why spending a little time designing your Avatar is crucial.

I will guide you through two new exercises now. Please follow them step by step as they will be crucial to success in your Identity Shift.

Just imagine yourself being a screenwriter of this 'amazing movie' you came up with in our previous chapter (your blueprint). Now that you have a rough idea of what the movie is going to be about you need to concentrate on your main character.

Imagine your favorite actor will be playing that role and it's crucial that they understand precisely who they need to become.

Step 1

Take a pen and paper (or a keyboard) and write down **everything** there is to know about that Avatar. Write a minimum of 100 one-word descriptions of the character traits your 'actor' will need to adjust to. Be extremely specific so your chosen actor will totally understand the role. The more precise you can be, the better this movie will play out.

Here are examples of my first 10 – although yours could be totally different.

1. Healthy
2. Powerful
3. Loving
4. Fun
5. Reliable
6. Confident
7. Creative
8. Funny
9. Decisive
10. Fearless

Keep going until you reach 100. I am not kidding – get it to 100!

Put yourself again in that 90-year-old body on a rocking chair from our previous chapters and get into that character. Who is THAT person?

That amazing person who lived that incredible life had four personality traits (based on Tony Robbins's archetypes). Tap into each one of them and ask for advice on what other character traits to add to your list.

The Warrior
What are the strength traits of your new Avatar? To be **that** 90-year-old person who lived this incredible life you described in your previous exercises, what warrior characteristics does your Avatar need?

The Lover
What are the loving and caring traits of the character? To be **that** person, what does your Avatar need?

The Magician
What are the resourceful traits of the character? To be **that** person, what does your Avatar need?

The Queen/The King
What are the noble traits of the character? To be **that** person, what does your Avatar need?

Keep writing until you get to at least 100. There is something about pushing yourself with writing. When you think you cannot come up with any more – perfect! Think of 20 more! Because that is when your subconscious mind goes, 'Holy shit, they are really serious about this.' The epiphanies you will come up with right at the end are the ones you will cherish most...

Stop reading now and go ahead, do the exercise – it's super important!

Step 2

Look at your list and **create a character** for each word. Pick a character which will appeal to you the most. For example, rather than just saying 'healthy', find a sexy label like 'fitness goddess', 'kick-butt athlete', 'snowboarder' or any others that you can think of. It will be whatever your ideal healthy and fit Avatar would be labeled as. You can also compare it with characters from movies.

Let's have some fun with this!

Here are some examples, but choose what works for you personally...

1. Healthy – Fitness God/ess
2. Powerful like Tarzan
3. LOVER like Marilyn Monroe
4. FUN – Surprise Master
5. Reliable – the Rock

6. Confident – the Boss
7. Creative – the Magician
8. Funny – Wit Master
9. Decisive – Ninja
10. Fearless – Bruce Lee

Step 3

Now that you have finished, take a new piece of paper and write at the top '**I AM**'.

You will find that the words 'I Am' are the most powerful words in your world because whatever you put after them will absolutely shape your destiny!

Everything that we are now going to write will be in the present tense and will start with 'I Am' statements.

Now, let's re-write the list again and then add a small paragraph to each description. Here are a few examples:

I AM creative like a **Magician** – I think outside the box and always come up with creative answers to my problems. Just like magic, answers always appear to me out of nowhere, delighting everybody around me. I always know what to do. I am super-creative!

I AM a **Fitness Goddess** – I look stunning and feel amazing. I always make the right choices when it comes to my health and fitness. I eat clean, I drink water, I move, I dance, I breathe deeply. My body is flexible like rubber, my skin is clear and soft, my eyes are bright with perfect 20/20 vision…etc.

I AM decisive like a **Ninja**. I take in all the information and make a decision immediately. I understand that progress means everything. If the decision turns out to be incorrect, it can be readjusted easily, but without making a decision nothing is ever achieved. I make my decisions in five seconds.

You can keep writing. My personal health section, for example, goes on for about two pages – covering everything from immaculate nails to cells regenerating through higher vibrations.

There is no restriction on how much you can write. Remember, the more precise you can be, the better your new Avatar will fit the role. Get super-creative with this one. Be the best screenwriter ever! Write like your life depends on it! Which it does...literally!

Go ahead and do this with your whole list. If you are having trouble with this, make sure you contact us through www.quantummindacademy.com.

OK, done?
Excellent!

Now, do yourself a favor and let's pretend you are that actor who is rehearsing for that role. For your new Avatar.

Get yourself to **read** with conviction all the words you have written down, starting each line with '**I AM**'. Make sure that you add the appropriate tone to each word. If you say 'compassionate', sound compassionate. If you say 'fun', sound fun! Read it aloud as if you were auditioning for the role. Make it real, make it powerful, make it CONVINCING!

Keep going…
And, when you finish, read it over again. Clearer. More convincing!

Keep those notes close to you – they will be useful when we get to the chapter on coding.

And always remember:

I AM – the two most powerful words, because what you put beside them will shape your destiny.

PART 4
Escaping Your Matrix
a.k.a.
Mission **Possible**

Can't Get You Out Of My Mind

OK, now that we know what it is that we want out of life, let's do some serious re-coding!

To be able to do that you need to understand how your subconscious mind works. A cute story written by Vince Poscente called 'The Ant and The Elephant' simplifies this a bit.

It compares the size of your conscious mind to an ant and your subconscious mind to an elephant. The story is about a little ant who wished to get to the oasis but discovers along the way that all the work he was doing trying to get there was useless because he lived on the back of an elephant – who happened to be walking in the totally *opposite* direction! The story then goes into teaching the ant how to speak the language of an elephant and turn it around. Obviously, with the leverage of a strong, powerful animal (the subconscious mind), achieving your goal of getting to the 'oasis' is so much quicker. It's a beautiful story, and I highly recommend reading it.

The trick is to realize that your conscious mind **needs** to learn how to speak to its subconscious 'elephant' as it's a totally different language that needs to be used. It's literally like the difference between Greek and Chinese – different grammar, different letters…different everything.

So let's figure this out. How do you talk to your subconscious mind? How do you communicate with this 'elephant of yours' so that it takes you to your own version of paradise?

Your conscious mind operates purely on logic and it tends to use words. Ever found your Siri 'yelling' at you for something that you have done? You are using WORDS.

Your subconscious mind has no idea what you are talking about. Ever! In fact, as cute as the comparison to an elephant is, we know from the previous chapters that your subconscious is a coding program and therefore doesn't even have anyone there to listen to you yell. There is no-one in there to hear you to change the coding – so stop pleading with yourself, yelling at yourself, getting annoyed with yourself and then even hating yourself for not having the 'willpower' to change. There is no-one on the other side to retrieve your message – however wonderful and helpful it might sound.

Here is what you need to know: your subconscious reacts to only IMAGES and FEELINGS. These two things are massively powerful to your subconscious as both trigger neuro-responses, which either move you forward or make you run.

Your thoughts appear in your mind as pictures. It's the pictures that your 'elephant' will follow. Always. In principle it sounds easy enough, but what we are forgetting is that we tend to focus on **negative stuff** more often than on **positive stuff.**

Unfortunately, your elephant does not register a 'no', an 'anti' or a 'don't'. If I were to say to you 'don't think of your house', there is no way of doing that. It's just physically impossible – you will visualize your house even though I said 'don't'. How many 'don'ts' do you have in your vocabulary?

Just imagine if you converted your current language into 'flash cards' for the subconscious to follow. What do you think the picture will be if you say, 'I can't eat doughnuts because I will get fat'? Yep, you've just flashed two powerful cards, one of you eating a doughnut and one of you being fat, and that is exactly the instructions you send to your subconscious to follow! You just told your subconscious that this is what you want!

In fact, the more emotion you add to that statement (e.g. anger), the brighter the pictures appear in your subconscious, speeding up your 'elephant' towards your 'goal'. In the previous example, rather than getting fit and avoiding fatty food, your 'elephant' will be racing towards all the doughnuts out there and getting you fatter and fatter. You can try to stop it with 'strong will' and, sure, you might succeed for a little while (while your 'elephant' throws some serious tantrums), but you and I both know that the minute you stop 'watching' your 'naughty elephant' it will make up for it. Ever been on a yo-yo diet? Hmmm...

This sort of language has always been misunderstood by humans. In fact, I sometimes wonder why it was invented in the first place. It's like telling Adam and Eve not to eat that apple – we all know how that story ended!

This whole concept of 'wrong flash cards' gets even more troublesome when our whole society starts using this language. Have you ever heard expressions like:

Anti-war rally
War on terror
War on guns
Anti-flu shot
Anti-gun

What pictures do you think are being flashed to people when using those words?

Do you think the cards flashed are congruent with what we're saying? Nope, they're very confusing and often attract the opposite to what we actually mean.

Mother Teresa is quoted to have said when once asked to participate in an anti-war demonstration:

'I will never do that!

But as soon as you have a pro-peace rally, I'll be there.'

Here is a woman who knew the power of language!

Always, **always** choose words which 'flash the right card'! It takes a little practice but before you know it you will be saying, 'I choose a healthy snack,' rather than saying, 'I can't eat that cake.'

Rather than saying 'I don't want to catch a cold,' say 'I'm always healthy' – it's the same meaning to the ant but what a **huge** difference to your elephant, as the pictures are **totally** different.

The word **'want'** is another one which will always trip you up. Imagine wanting something. Really wanting it. Begging for it. What images do you see in your mind? We are all different, but I see a person down on their knees lamenting with their hands up – a rather grim picture, if I say so. Did you get something similar?

Now, if you were to place the word 'want' into a sentence like 'I want to be rich,' you will get two flash cards: a beggar and a rich card (whatever the word 'rich' looks like for you). And so your 'elephant' goes, 'OK, the boss [you] wants to spend their life on their knees begging [want card] for riches [rich card]' – done! Can you see how that can be easily misunderstood?

When you want something or someone you are flashing a powerful card to your subconscious mind that this is your goal. The WANTING becomes your goal. You will forever get stuck in the loop of wanting **whatever the second card shows. You don't want to be rich – you are rich!**

Life's biggest irony is that, the richer you **want** to become, the poorer you will feel; the more beautiful you **want** to become, the uglier you will feel; the more successful you **want** to become, the more like a failure you will feel. Why? Because you use the word '**want**'. You are using the flash card of a 'beggar who is lacking something', and so the subconscious, like the faithful servant, delivers more of...WANTING!

Ask and you shall receive – someone famous once said. ☺

This is why we have used the words 'I am' in our exercises in previous chapters. '**I am** healthy', NOT '**I want** to be healthy' – please understand how **crucial** this is. Not only does the word 'want' come with a negative picture; it also carries a terrible feeling – a feeling of lacking something. Remember how we talked about each thought being like a two-sided coin? That it always has a feeling on the other side? This is why 'want' should be avoided at all costs. Replace it with the feeling of abundance.

If you flash cards which are showing that you are rich – in present tense and embodying the feeling that comes with it – that is what the elephant will run towards. If you embody the feeling of being lovable right now, people will automatically be attracted to you. Never work this magic in reverse by throwing a negative card into the mix!

All successful people realize the power of images. Clarity is the key. In fact, your subconscious mind **does not** know the difference between reality and imagination, which is superb because now you are in control of what pictures you'd like to feed your subconscious mind.

It's also crucial to remember that your subconscious is not that good with abstract words. You cannot just say, 'I am happy,' and expect that your subconscious will know exactly what you mean. It will quit pursuing the goal as soon as it thinks it's reached it. How will your subconscious know that you have reached your goal? Treat your subconscious mind like a five year old – they are very, very literal. What sorts of feelings will you feel when you are happy? What will you see? Be specific.

What will you hear other people saying when you have accomplished your goal? What will you say to yourself? Use some future quotes.

How will you feel when you accomplish your goal?
Remember the feeling of achievement from the past? Try to recollect exactly what it felt like. Where in the body did you feel that feeling?

The thing is, the more precise you can be with your vision, the clearer the 'flash card' will appear. Use these kinds of descriptions for every category listed in your blueprint.

The most successful Olympic athletes use visualization as part of their training. Some even include – you guessed it – virtual reality training. The more you can feed your mind crystal-clear images of achievement, the more familiar it will become. The more familiar it is, the more your elephant runs towards it.

All you need is vision, clarity and emotion. The more positive the emotion you attach to the image you create, the more 'realistic' it becomes to your subconscious. If you can imagine drawing a new neuropathway in your mind, adding emotion to it is like painting over a pencil sketch with a thick texta: one is more powerful, and clearer, than the other.

Clear Picture + Strong Emotion = Faster Impact!

In addition to changing our way of consciously dealing with internal linguistics, we need to develop a foolproof way of communicating with our subconscious mind, and simply relying on positive thinking will not be enough.

We need to get right into the subconscious!

As we talked about in previous chapters, the majority of what you have learned came to you before the age of seven as your brain functioned on a theta level brain vibration frequency. This was prior to your having any ability to reason. When someone told you that you were 'no good' at something, you didn't analyze why they said it – you just accepted it as truth and took it at face value.

If you saw an unhealthy relationship between your parents, boom, you accepted it as a role model for your future self. Whether it was healthy or not, you just took it in as a given – everything got written straight into your program to forever create a blueprint for your life. Sucks, I know!

Kids up to the age of seven live in the state of theta brain vibration when awake, and they constantly mix reality and imagination. This is why they often ride their unicorns or become superheroes: their imagination is in overdrive.

But there is good news: theta level is also the level of hypnosis. In adulthood, it's that twilight state which we normally experience only momentarily as we wake or drift off to sleep – you know, the state when you are not sure if you are in a dream or awake, the state where you combine reality and imagination and when you fully wake up you ask yourself, 'Did that actually happen?'

Knowing that we have access to this level of vibration every single day is super important because it's a state that bypasses your reasoning self. This is the time when magic happens, and harnessing this time for coding is essential. You just need to have a self-hypnosis recording which you can listen to as you fall asleep or as soon as you wake up.

It's critical to bypass the reasoning self because, if you would like to code something that isn't a reality at this stage, your conscious mind will 'argue with you'. If you say, 'I am fit and healthy,' your Siri will just say, "Yeah, right!" and throw you a bunch of examples of why it's not true. You must bypass that little 'smart gatekeeper'.

I personally find that listening to a recording of your **own voice** is so much more powerful than using an off-the-shelf product. Although they might be nice and fancy with beautiful voices, it's a stranger's voice coding you – which makes your conscious mind curious. When it's your own voice – even a DIY recording – it doesn't seem to raise any curiosity; it just lets it in straight past 'the gates' because it recognizes itself in it.

We will discuss in further chapters how you can create your own custom-made self-hypnosis recording.

The other powerful way for your subconscious to learn is by repetition. Let's face it, that is how we have been learning ever since our reasoning years. This is how we learned to ride a bike, learned our ABCs, poems and lyrics to our favorite songs. Repeat, repeat, repeat.

When you first learned how to drive a car, **everything** was a conscious effort. Look at this mirror, look at the other mirror, look out for pedestrians, look out for other cars, put a blinker on, press a pedal – the whole lot was a conscious resolve. But, after doing it enough times, it got engraved into your subconscious mind (known as a habit) so much so that you now do all these actions without even thinking. Sometimes you leave a place and then wonder how on earth you got home – your subconscious was doing the driving on its own while entertaining you with thoughts from the past (memories) or sending you into the future by projecting itself into some new situations – also via thoughts…

If you use the tools for self-hypnosis, eventually the program will create space in your subconscious mind for it and it WILL become your new habit. As the mind is obsessed with coherency, it will automatically look for ways of 'proving itself right', thus it will automatically adjust your behaviors and start noticing things which will be in line with the new program. You won't have to strain yourself to change behaviors by yelling at yourself or wasting your conscious mind on positive thinking; you will become your new custom-made, upgraded and improved self.

Coding 101 For 'Dummies'

OK, are you ready for this? Are you ready to do some serious re-coding?

We will create your self-made, hypnotic recordings with appropriate sound in the background to help you get into the right state straightaway.

This chapter will guide you through three different recordings, each one with different brain waves, to be listened to at different optimal times.

Let me explain those brain waves a little more for you.

Your brain operates on different frequencies:

Delta frequency – deep sleep 'recharging your batteries', healing, pain relief
Theta frequency – is the hypnotic state of almost being asleep but not quite
Alpha frequency – is your relaxed, effortless, flow state; super-creative
Beta frequency – problem solving, analytical, focused attention
Gamma frequency – memory recall, peak awareness, high-level information processing

Below are instructions on how to create your own DIY recordings at absolutely zero cost.

You will need the following items:

A computer with Internet connection
Your blueprint
Your Avatar
Smartphone with recording app
Watch (a stopwatch is best)

To make your recordings we need to do the following six things – please follow these instructions to a T as these will be the seeds for your transformation.

Blueprint

Make sure you have your full blueprint ready. Read through it carefully, category by category. Make sure everything in it resonates with you. Ensure that everything is how you want it to play out. There must be plenty of WHAT and plenty of WHY – just stay away from HOW. The subconscious mind – that elephant of yours – is quite stubborn. It doesn't like being told how to do things. It just needs to have a crystal-clear picture of what feelings you want to experience. Make it all in present tense.

Avatar

You will also need your journal notes on the character we have created in the chapter on your Avatar. Read through it carefully and make sure you are happy with it. See how your Avatar relates to your blueprint. Remember, to achieve things in your blueprint your character has to match the task ahead. There's not much point in choosing a fat, lazy and sloppy actor to play an action hero – if you know what I mean.

Theta Waves Music

Now, let's get to choosing your background music. What we will be looking for are theta waves. From a coding and re-coding perspective, theta vibrations are of the highest interest to us. They take you straight into a hypnotic trance, which means they will help you get through the gates of your subconscious much more quickly.

You can find free theta music on YouTube. Just open your Google search and type in 'theta music youtube'. It will come up with a range of different sounds. Try out a few and find one that resonates with you. Listen to it for a while and make sure it doesn't contain sounds that you find annoying. The more attractive the sound to you, the more your subconscious will enjoy this.

Smartphone and a Watch

OK, now pull out your phone, set it on 'recording'.

On your computer, press 'play' on the music from YouTube.

Press record on your phone.

Make sure the music is loud but not uncomfortable.

Sit approximately half a meter from your computer speakers.

Keep an eye on your watch (a stopwatch is best).

Imagine you are the actor you have chosen to play your role. Read the blueprint you created in the voice of that actor – confident, deliberate and animated.

Allow one minute of the music to play from the beginning – then start reading.

Allow seven seconds between statements or sentences. This will allow your subconscious to flash all the required images for each statement.

Try to stretch the recording to approximately 30 minutes – if it turns out to be shorter, read it again until you have a full 30-minute recording.

Once finished, name the recording 'Deep Hypnosis'.

Now we will prepare a recording which you can use during the day. Go and find your favorite upbeat song on YouTube, adding 'karaoke' at the end of your search. Make sure it's a song which you would use if you were walking fast or running. My favorite is 'Flaunt it' by TV Rock – it doesn't really matter what song you use as long as it has a similar fast beat.

The karaoke version will give you an instrumental version only (with no lyrics). You will create your own lyrics by re-reading your Avatar statements from your journal. This time the reading must be more upbeat – in line with the song's beat. The more fun you make it, the more your subconscious will enjoy it. Just read the Avatar blueprint.

Once completed, save the recording as 'Fast-Paced Coding'.

Now we are going to prepare a recording which will get through to you during the day while your mind is active. As the conscious mind is always on high alert, it's a little harder to get through 'the gates' of your ego. When you are wide awake, if you make the statement 'I am sexy', your smart-ass Siri will just respond, 'Hahaha, yeah, right! What about the…'
There is, however, a way of getting around that protective little program, and that is by using what's called a 'lofty question', a technique used by one of the most successful Hollywood

hypnotherapists, Christie Marie Sheldon.

This time, instead of making a statement, you will turn it into a question. As your mind cannot perform two tasks at the same time, it will get tricked into fetching the right pictures. Rather than just saying 'I am sexy', turn it into the question, 'Why am I so sexy?' And so on.

Be creative with this one. Whatever you ask, your subconscious mind will automatically default into fetching ALL the reasons why you are right – BOOM!

As this recording will be played only during the day, when your mind is active, its background music will have to be in alpha vibrations. **Alpha** is known to boost accelerated learning, and works in the relaxed, flow state. It's ideal music for contemplating why you are so sexy. Or smart. Or wealthy. Or whatever you choose to contemplate.

Go ahead and find yourself 'alpha vibrations music' on YouTube. This time choose 30-50 of your best statements and read them as a question with real curiosity.

Here are some examples, but get creative with this and come up with your own:

'Why am I always surrounded by love?'
'Why do people find me so attractive?'
'Why are my friends so generous?'
'Why am I such a brilliant writer?'
'Why is everybody smiling at me?'
'Why is my life so amazing?'

You get the picture...

I trust you have completed your recordings. If you haven't, please do them now as they are crucial to your success and I really don't want this to be just another book you read and forget – we have to get the results for you!

So, go on – do it!

If you have completed your recordings, you should have three of them:

Deep Hypnosis – with theta waves
Fast-Paced Coding – with your favorite fast soundtrack
Lofty Questions – with alpha waves

NOW, this is how you use them.

Deep Hypnosis is the most important recording you have made – it's a recording you will listen to **every night** and **every morning**. First, you'll listen to it just before you fall asleep, and then as soon as you wake up. This is super important!

Set an alarm for half an hour before you need to get up and put your earphones on. You might find yourself falling asleep. This is OK; theta waves are very relaxing, and your subconscious mind never switches off. All you are doing is getting around your reasoning mind and your ego, and throwing your 'brilliant pictures' straight into the coding brain.

Fast-Paced Coding – Sometime during the day (choose your own time) head out the door and do some walking. I am sure your health and fitness section had some requirement for movement. It doesn't matter whether it's a walk around the block, walking to the shops, walking the dog or a jog, choose brisk movement every day. Pop your headphones on, put your **Fast-Paced Coding** on repeat. Do at least 30 minutes of walking every day. And if you don't think you have the time – well, find it! The quality of your future life depends on it!

Lofty Questions can be listened to during a work break or any other break you might have. I like to listen to mine after breakfast to have my mind contemplating my 'sexiness' or 'intelligence' throughout the day ☺. It's kinda fun! My mind also contemplates what new million-dollar idea I can manifest today and why people around me are so generous and loving. I love it!

Those lofty questions are so powerful – what they are doing is reframing your day. Remember how in our earlier chapters we talked about your mind being hit with over two million bits of information per second? Well, what lofty questions do is filter through those info bits to take in **only** stuff which supports your questions. How cool is that?

In addition to listening to your lofty questions via your recording, you will end up learning them off by heart. Eventually, start asking yourself those questions randomly throughout the day.

The best thing about what you have just created is that no-one needs to know about it. You don't need to announce anything, you don't have to go anywhere, you don't need to spend any money – all you have to do is commit to listening to your recordings.

Once you read through this book and complete your recordings, I challenge you to a 30-day re-coding – I promise you, your life will never be the same!

PART 5
Life Beyond 'The Matrix'

Follow The 'White Rabbit'

The brilliant thing about your subconscious mind – that proverbial elephant of yours – is that, as long as it knows what it is you are looking for, it will find the best way to get it. The only thing it requires you to do is **trust it** and it will get you there and then 'get out of its way'. Even if you feel like it might be going off course, just trust it. It knows the best way – in ways that you have never even imagined.

This is sometimes easier said than done, but you have to understand that, the minute you start interfering and micromanaging **how** you want the Universe or the subconscious mind to deliver your wishes, you are literally sending it a signal that you don't trust it; and that's throwing your 'beggar card' into the mix again and attracting more wanting, needing and anxiety.

Your job (your conscious mind's), the 'ant's' job, is to figure out **what** your 'oasis' looks like (which we have done through our recordings) and have a big enough WHY – excitement within – so that your 'elephant' confidently runs towards the goals.

Just look back on your life. Have you ever had a big goal which you achieved but in a totally different way to how you thought you would? In fact, you got there in a way you could never have predicted? The chances are you will get 100% of what you wish for through the pictures you are flashing, but the means by which you get 99% of it will be a surprise. This is simply how the Universe works – so stop predicting stuff and overthinking the HOW. That's not your job! Just trust that everything is happening for a reason and somehow in the future it will make a lot of sense. The dots will connect. They always do.

You cannot and should not control the narrative of the movie/game you are in. Just think about it – it would be totally boring if you did. If you could predict everything that happened to you, what would be the point? Would you really enjoy watching a movie which was 100% predictable from the beginning to the end *and* you knew all the lines too? Of course not! We love movies that surprise us. We enjoy movies that have a great balance of ups and downs, of sadness and laughter, of predictability and adventure, of bravery and adversity. Movies that move us, movies that make us cry **and** make us laugh! Movies that make us FEEL human!

Here you are in the middle of one of those movies – an absolutely brilliant virtual reality game of life – except now you have the power to choose what genre that movie/game is. Is your life going to be an adventure? A tragedy? A comedy? A tale of a hero? A crime story? A love story? If you were telling somebody the story of your life at the age of 90, what genre would you label it?

Once your subconscious is given direction (through your recordings) your only job now is to say yes to the future 'dots'. 'Follow the white rabbit' is a famous quote from the movie The Matrix. If something you spot makes you curious or excites you and it resonates with your blueprint, **follow it** and embrace the journey. There is a reason why it's showing up. Be brave and follow the 'white rabbit' even if the path is unknown.

It's especially important to take action. If something out there interests you, open that door. Find out more. Follow it. It could be as simple as a Google search. A small connection. An email sent. Just…something. Don't let it sit idle without taking action. Your job is to ensure that your elephant is always on the move.

My most bizarre 'follow the rabbit' experience happened a few years ago after I wrote down that I would like to meet Oprah Winfrey. Now, that's a big statement considering she is super-famous, she lives on the other side of the globe and of course half of the world would like to meet her. The crazy thing is I got to meet her within 10 days of writing down this goal. A person I hadn't seen for about five years posted on Facebook that Oprah was coming to Australia and she was looking for someone to go with her to Oprah's event. I had no idea Oprah was coming to Australia. I soon found out there were going to be 5,000 attendees, so I told my friend I wouldn't go because there wasn't much chance of meeting her. All the 'meet and greet' tickets were sold out two months prior. As I closed off that door, I remembered the rule to always take some 'towards' action, however small…

So I emailed Oprah's management company in Chicago and told them how I'd missed out on VIP tickets and asked them to please let me know if anyone dropped out. I seriously wasn't expecting a response. **However**, the day before Oprah's show I received a phone call from Chicago asking me if I still wanted to go as two major attendees just happened to drop out. My friend and I got to meet and talk to Oprah, hang out with her for a couple of hours and see her show from the first row at the stadium. Now, that's the power of the Universe. There is no way I could have planned this any better. Always, always follow the 'white rabbit' even if it seems unreachable.

Life's stories are studded with mysterious coincidences, serendipities, off-chance meetings, missed trains, overheard conversations, a meeting of eyes across a crowded room – so you need to develop the ability to act on your curiosities.

When you get the hang of this, you will be able to recognize these 'dots' as synchronicities which are suddenly appearing. You will wonder how you have never seen them in the past. They came as messages from The Universal Mind and not our own reasoning mind. They just naturally appear at the back of our minds, and they seem almost too random, too spontaneous and not that logical at first. But if you ask yourself, 'Why did I think of this now,' suddenly you will receive an answer that makes perfect sense: 'Follow it! That's your "white rabbit".'

Synchronicities also come in the form of wise words of another human being. Have you ever had a question on your mind and then suddenly you meet somebody who can answer it for you? Yes, chances are you probably googled it first, but somehow you've ended up talking with people who were also on the same wavelength. These are not coincidences – this happens by design!

The moment you open your heart to your intuition, the signs will show up.

And, if you would like to speed up the process of those coincidences, here is how you do it...

Uplift the energy of everybody who comes into your life. Add consciousness to every human interaction from now on. Look people in the eye and see their soul rather than a body. Your energy will uplift theirs and open up a communication channel to hear more synchronicity. You will be 'mind-blown' by this!

Once you decide on the direction, leave the rest to the more than capable Universe (a.k.a. producer) to fill in the blanks. That's the only way you will get to enjoy your own life.

Always remember to invest yourself in the **process**, not the outcome.

You can't control the outcome, but you also do not know what other doors your activities will open up. Sometimes what seems like a bad thing will turn out to be the greatest thing ever, as it opens doors to other opportunities which eventually lead to your desired outcome. Go with the flow – detach yourself from the outcome.

Have you ever noticed that, when you are negotiating with someone **and** you are willing to walk away because you are not dependent on the outcome, you always have the upper hand and often you get what you want? Life just works like that: if you are chasing something, it will run away; but, if you are willing to walk away, it will find you – if it's meant for you. Just trust that whatever happens for you is happening for a reason. As mentioned before, the dots will eventually connect. They always do.

Flashlight Theory

Your awareness is like a flashlight: it lights up where you point it. Shine it at a wall and it will light up the wall, shine it at a car and you will see the car. Become aware of where you are pointing your light. Your subconscious gets attracted to it and assumes that's where you want to go. It's like a crazy baby elephant with ears flapping chasing your laser beam light – so make sure you point it towards only what you enjoy the most.

The best way of shining your light on what you want is through celebrating what you already have. This is the best clue for the subconscious to bring you more. Gratitude is the key. Look around at what you already have in your life and be super-grateful for it. Again, the clarity and emotions are crucial.

Have you ever bought something for a friend and they were much more excited about and thankful for it than you expected them to be? So much so that it made you feel warm and fuzzy inside? That gratefulness makes you want to go back and get them even more stuff because you would like to experience that pleasure of giving and gratitude again and again. That is how your proverbial elephant feels. If you are grateful for your generous friends, it will get you more generosity. If you are grateful for the clothes on your back, the subconscious will get you more and better clothes. If you are grateful for your car, it will get you one that's even better. If you are grateful for the love in your relationship, it will strengthen it even more. Whatever you are grateful for, even if what you currently have might not yet be the best, shine a light on it, feel the gratitude and 'watch your elephant' fetch you more of what you like!

One of the best hacks I use to remember to be grateful is every time I see a red car driving past I say, 'I am so grateful for (insert your own gratitude),' and embrace the feeling of gratefulness. You can use whatever reminder you like; this one seems to work for me. It will become a habit before you know it.

Our world depends on people like you – people who have awakened and are willing to take their journey into their own hands. Some people are ready to be 'tapped on the shoulder', some are not. Embrace your own journey, and when you start becoming a shining example of what's possible people will ask you how. Give them this book as a gift and watch them stop, take off their 'VR mask' and smile back at you with understanding. This is the coolest thing you'll ever experience, especially if these are people close to you!

Meanwhile, as Mahatma Gandhi once said, 'Be the Change you want to see in the World.'

7 Wisdoms To Live By

Here are the most important takeaways from this book:

1. **Outgrow your NEED.** Understand that the 'flash card' for **want** and **need** is one of the most harmful cards you can play. Concentrate on BEING. Embody your Avatar fully. You cannot attract change into your life by remaining the same person driven by the same ego. Your ego needs to evolve into your new Avatar. Be who you have imagined. Take that proverbial 'virtual reality mask' off from time to time and ask yourself, 'WHO AM I BEING in this game of life?' Sometimes your new Avatar needs to take a breather – take time out and re-evaluate your role. If you don't like who you are being, re-code it!

2. **Be aware of your 'customized Siri' and the internal mental chatter your ego indulges in.** Always remember that whatever your ANT says is flashed in pictures for the ELEPHANT – so make sure that those pictures are crystal clear, in present tense and positively reflect your request. Add some good feeling and enough WHY so that the elephant gets excited about getting you to your 'oasis'.

3. **Your awareness is like a flashlight.** Live in constant gratitude for what you have in your life which you enjoy. Choose a reminder that will trigger you to make a statement about what you are grateful for. The more you appreciate what you have, the more and better of it you will get.

4. **Focus on the process, not the outcome.** Put emotion and energy into the action you are taking to achieve your goals. It's always about the journey, not the destination. The purpose of achieving is not the goal itself – it's the learning and the growth that happens to you, and for you, while you are taking action. The destination is a mirage: you get there and you will want something different. It's the journey that you need to enjoy – and, when you lose attachment to the outcome, the probability of your achieving it increases.

5. **Know that all that happens, happens for a reason.** It's neither good nor bad – it just is. Don't put meaning to your experiences. Have you had something happen to you that was terrible at the time and then turned out to be the greatest thing that ever happened to you? The dots always connect – always look at things that happen as a positive step to get you towards your 'oasis'. The Universe has a real sense of humor and might take you on an unexpected adventure, but be assured that what you seek shall be found.

6. **Chase your coincidences and synchronicities like Pokémon.**
Always take action, however small, and follow that 'white rabbit'. There are no coincidences – these are markers for you to follow to get you to where you are heading. If your compass is well aligned and set on your true North Star (by coding your blueprint to your subconscious), all there is left is moving forward. Remember, nothing in life is static – you either grow or you die. Always choose growth.

7. **Live in the NOW.** There is no past and there is no future in your virtual game of life. There is only NOW. Understand that the illusion of the past and the illusion of the future have been created only so that you get attached to the character/avatar you play. Without the story of the past, your old ego cannot exist. You can literally change the meaning of all your past experiences by changing the story attached to your experiences – and just like that you become a different person. It's like walking in a mirror maze. Everything outside of present tense is an illusion. The more energy and consciousness you put into doing every activity in the NOW, the more control you will have over how your life unfolds. Set a whole bunch of alarms on your smartphone to go off at random times to remind you to get back into present time. Pay attention to the texture and colors of the leaves on trees you pass by – they will bring you to the now. And, if in distress, always remember to 'pull that mask off' and breathe – it's just a game!

With A Little Help From My Friends

Let's continue this journey together.

Here is YOUR MISSION, SHOULD YOU CHOOSE TO ACCEPT IT.

I dare you to take this 45-day challenge of designing your blueprint and re-coding your subconscious mind to follow your Life's Purpose.

15 days to read this book and finish your journal, and
30 days of re-coding!

I can't wait to hear what results and synchronicities you will encounter.

Send me an email at anna@quantummindacademy.com or comment on our Facebook page to let me know what transformations you have been able to achieve!

And for those of you who would like to continue this journey together, here are a few ways you can do this:

I have started Quantum Mind Academy as a place where my readers can be supported in being able to successfully re-code their subconscious minds. If you feel that after reading this book you are still not quite confident in taking this journey on your own, be assured that there is plenty of help!

A community of likeminded people awaits you.

There is an online course which will guide you through the process of defining your purpose, blueprint creation, avatar creation and preparation of your own hypnosis recordings.

I know how easy it is to slip back into old habits. Or, worse, read the book and promise yourself that you will get around to doing the exercises, only to find years down the track that life again got in the way!

If you haven't done the exercises, you know exactly what I mean.

By the time you finish the online course you will know your purpose and you will have everything ready to plug into your ears for great re-coding. I will even give you some cheat sheets with my own personal scripts to use however you wish!

And those of you who would like to take it a notch higher and would like to ensure success, why not join our **12-month Quantum Mastermind**?

I have designed it specifically for those who are **really** ready for change.

I have found with some of my past clients that they start with great intentions but somewhere along the way they get sidetracked. If you are really serious about mastering this Game of Life – come and join us!

Our Mastermind is the best accountability group you will ever experience. Not only do we expand on each category every single month, but we give each other support and hold each other accountable to the promises we make to ourselves and to the group.

I am one of those individuals who is obsessed with learning and implementation. I track down the best specialists in the world in each blueprint category and often take courses, or 1:1 training, which are thousands of dollars in value.

Every month we will discuss a different category and I will give you a rundown of the best techniques and concepts I have ever come across. We then discuss any other ideas of how else we could improve on that particular category. The session ends with everybody making some kind of commitment about what strategy they would like to implement that best fits their lifestyle. Everyone is unique and will have different goals, however the facilitation of this Mastermind will ensure that your goals are actual 'end goals' – quantifiable and true to your soul.

Throughout the month we have a private Facebook group where we pledge our commitments, cheer each other on and celebrate our successes.

As a habit usually takes 28 days to form, by the time we get to our next category you will have installed some brilliant habits already. Each month will come with new recordings for you to install and lots of inspiration.

Think of this Mastermind like a group of friends sitting by a fire – when your own fire diminishes, you get it re-ignited by the group. You don't have to go through this alone!! Let's see what synchronicities we can create together!

Before you're accepted into the Mastermind, you will be invited to have a 1:1 session to make sure that your blueprint and coding have been done exactly the way you would like them to be and that you are really following your purpose. Only those who are really seeking a real improvement will be accepted into the group.

Check our website www.mastermindacademy.com for our next intake.

And, lastly, if you would like to help people around you be enlightened, give them a gift of this book. Rather than trying to explain it to them, let them take their own 'virtual reality' masks off.

I find this book opens up conversations which are sometimes hard to have. Let this be your gift to someone who needs awakening! For the price of a book, you can change someone's life. Spread the joy around!!

You can order this book in hard copy or as an ebook or audiobook – just follow the links on our website.

I hope to see you one day in our Quantum Tribe and meet you face to face. Whichever way you chose to go, I wish you much happiness on your own journey to fulfillment!!

Let your Energy Shine!!!

Love

Anna

Glossary
of weird and wonderful words used in this book:

Avatar – in the gaming world it is a fictional character you choose to become. In this book Avatar refers to the upgrade of your own character.

Attachment Theory – began in the 1950s and has since accumulated considerable research behind it. Two researchers named Bowlby and Ainsworth found that the way in which infants get their needs met by their parents significantly contributes to their 'attachment strategy' throughout their lives in adult relationships.

Aunties with mustaches – sad attempt at humour, a weird relative

Blueprint – a plan for your whole life

Brain Frequencies – The EEG (electroencephalograph) measures brainwaves of different frequencies within the brain. Electrodes are placed on specific sites on the scalp to detect and record the electrical impulses within the brain.

- **Delta frequency** – is found in deep sleep when 'recharging your batteries', healing, pain relief
- **Theta frequency** – is the hypnotic state of almost being asleep but not quite
- **Alpha frequency** – is your relaxed, effortless, flow state; super-creative
- **Beta frequency** – problem solving, analytical, focused attention
- **Gamma frequency** – memory recall, peak awareness, high-level information processing

Confirmation Bias – is the tendency to search for, interpret, favor, and recall information in a way that confirms or supports one's prior beliefs or values.

Conscious Mind – Your thinking, reasoning mind

Ego – a character you developed which holds back emotions you weren't allowed to experience as a child

Lofty Questions – a technique used by one of the most successful Hollywood hypnotherapists, Christie Marie Sheldon. It turns statements into questions.

NLP, Neuro Linguistic Programming – is a pseudoscientific approach to communication, personal development, and psychotherapy created by Richard Bandler and John Grinder in California, United States, in the 1970s.

Pokémon – are virtual characters in a cell phone game which project onto a real street. It was originally developed in Japan to promote physical activity and by 2019 had over a billion users worldwide. People ran down streets to find their Pokémon, which gave them points. It got so ridiculous that all you saw were people walking down streets constantly looking at their phones to locate their Pokémon. Some governments eventually banned the game because there were too many accidents – some players were hit by cars, others fell off cliffs. All in the name of a game.

Siri / Customized Siri – a metaphor for your internal voice (being compared to the voice on an Apple mobile device)

Subconscious Mind – the part of your mind that is responsible for running your body. It also stores your memories and emotions.

The Matrix - in this book is the conditioning of your mind or a restrictive program – it is the limit of your current thinking.

3 Principles: The late Sydney Banks first introduced these principles – the Principle of Universal Mind, the Principle of Consciousness and the Principle of Thought – to the world in the 1970s as a way of understanding the human experience. An ordinary man working as a welder at the time but who went on to become a well-known philosopher and author, Banks had what he described as an experience of profound spiritual enlightenment. It was an insight into our true nature as human beings and the process of how we experience life. It revealed a deeper truth about how life works and who and what we are.

Virtual Reality – the computer-generated simulation of a three-dimensional image or environment that can be interacted with in a seemingly real or physical way by a person using special electronic equipment, such as a helmet with a screen inside or gloves fitted with sensors. In this book Virtual Reality refers to the Life as you know it.

Sources of Inspiration and Wisdom

Whilst these are the resources I have referred to throughout this book, there are many sources and inspirations I have drawn from along this journey.

I am so grateful to all the authors, trainers and teachers, past and present, who have opened my mind to the possibilities of abundant life and who no doubt will inspire others as well.

Recommended Books

Brach, Ph.D, Tara: Radical Acceptance

Bradshaw, John: Creating Love: A New Way of Understanding Our Most Important Relationships

Bradshaw, John: Healing the Shame That Binds You

Bradshaw, John: Homecoming: Reclaiming and Healing Your Inner Child

Brown, Ph.D, Brené: The Power of Vulnerability

Byrne, Rhonda: The Secret

Chopra, M.D., Deepak: Ageless Body, Timeless Mind

Chopra, M.D., Deepak: Meta Human

Chopra, M.D., Deepak: Quantum Healing

Chopra, M.D., Deepak: Synchrodestiny

Chopra, M.D., Deepak: Unconditional Life

Chopra, M.D., Deepak: You Are the Universe

Cialdini, Ph.D, Robert: Influence

Dispenza, Dr Joe: Becoming Supernatural

Dispenza, Dr Joe: Breaking the Habit of Being Yourself

Dispenza, Dr Joe: Evolve Your Brain

Dispenza, Dr Joe: You Are The Placebo

Gilbert, Elizabeth: Big Magic

Goleman, Daniel: Emotional Intelligence

Hamilton, Roger: Your Life Your Legacy

Hawkeye, Timber: Buddhist Boot Camp

Heath, Chip & Heath, Dan: The Power of Moments

Hicks, Esther & Hicks, Jerry: The Astonishing Power Of Emotions

Kaku, Michio: Parallel Worlds

Kaku, Michio: Physics of The Impossible
Kaku, Michio: The Future of Humanity

Kaku, Michio: The Future of The Mind

Lakhiani, Vishen: The Code of the Extraordinary Mind

Lipton, Ph.D., Bruce H: Spontaneous Evolution

Lipton, Ph.D., Bruce H: The Biology of Belief

Lipton, Ph.D., Bruce H: The Honeymoon Effect

Manson, Mark: The Subtle Art of Not Giving A F*ck

Murphy, Ph.D., D.D., Joseph: The Power of Your Subconscious Mind

Neill, Michael: Inside Out Revolution

Neill, Michael: Supercoach

Pearson, Sharon: Ultimate You

Poscente, Vince: The Ant and The Elephant

Revel, Jean-François and Ricard, Matthieu – The Monk and The Philosopher

Robbins, Anthony: Awaken The Giant Within
Robbins, Mel: Take Control of Your Life

Satir, Virginia: Satir Model

Satir, Virginia: The New Peoplemaking

Satir, Virginia: Your Many Faces: Your First Step To Being Loved

Seip, Roger & Zbierski, Robb: Master Your Mind

Seligman, Ph.D., Martin E.P: Authentic Happiness

Tolle, Eckhart: The Power Of Now

Walsch, Neale Donald: Conversation With God 1, 2 and 3

Williams, Robert M: Psych-K. The Missing Peace In Your Life

Wright, Avery: Cognitive Behavioral Therapy

Wright, Avery: Neuro-Linguistic Programming

Wright, Avery: Psychology of Human Behavior, Emotional Intelligence

Recommended Training / Quests

Banks, Sydney: 3 Principles

Beckwith, Michael: Life Visioning Mastery. Mindvalley

Butcher, Jon and Missy: Lifebook. Mindvalley

Peer, Marisa: Rapid Transformational Hypnotherapy. Mindvalley

Peer, Marisa: Uncompromised Life. Mindvalley

Robbins, Anthony: Date With Destiny

Robbins, Anthony: Life Mastery

Robbins, Anthony: Unleash the Power Within

Sharma, Robin: Hero, Genius, Legend. Mindvalley

Walsch, Neale Donald: Awaken The Species. Mindvalley

Recommended Documentaries:

Byrne, Rhonda: The Secret

Samadhi Movie 2017

What The Bleep Do We Know?

About the Author:

Before my first near-death experience, my life was a series of 'proving myself to the world'.

Proving to my parents that I am independent and smart.
Proving that I can survive a refugee camp in a foreign country.
Proving to my ex-boyfriend that I can live without him after I was cheated on. Proving I can become wealthy on my own.

My mind was always wired for 'proving something to the world'.

So you can imagine what happened when, at the age of 23, I met a property developer who told me I would never make it in real estate because I was female, I was too young and I was blond (whatever that meant): I took it like a red flag to a bull and...spent the next 15 years proving *him* wrong!

I built an empire. I started with nothing and became a property developer involved in projects with over 4,500 homes. I lived on a beautiful farm, drove fancy cars, flew to projects by helicopter, and worked with people twice my age and 10 times as smart. In the eyes of the public and thousands of clients I 'had it all'.

But what they didn't see were the realities and stresses of competitive business: the sleepless nights, the juggling of massive mortgages, the 'secret boys' club' I would never belong to and the 'dog-eat-dog' politics involved.

And, since I would never back down, my work took over my life. After all, I had to 'prove *him* wrong'!

See, in the eyes of society I was experiencing success – but what was happening under the hood was a totally different story.

I missed my first wedding anniversary dinner because I was too busy running a meeting – and so I forgot – leaving my husband to eat dinner by himself while watching candles melt.

If we ever took a holiday, it was somewhere with a tropical view, watching our kids play while I was on the phone with lawyers closing deals and negotiating contracts.

My health was also in a shambles. One day my bank required me to have insanely high life insurance to cover their risk. It required medical tests, so I went to the doctor and he put me on a treadmill. I was told I needed to lose weight to be insured. I was in only my mid-30s.

Who knows how much longer I would have kept going to 'prove something to the world' if it weren't for the Universe 'bursting my superficial bubble'.

When my business was going through the toughest time and my laser focus was on not losing it all, we experienced one of the biggest fires in Australian history. During one of our scorching hot Australian summers, fire snuck up on us while we were inside – kids watching a video, me on the phone – all isolated by heavy curtains and the sound of an air conditioner, oblivious to what was going on outside.

When we finally realized the fires were close, I grabbed my four- and five-year-old little girls, one under each arm, shoved them into my car and drove through paddocks to get away from the 10-story high wall of fire racing our way – all this whilst watching in my rearview mirror my husband and neighbors staying back to rescue some show horses and other animals we had on our farm.

It took almost half an hour, which felt like a lifetime, before I got a phone call from my husband that they made it out alive and everybody was safe. I pulled off to the side of the road and had a total meltdown. For the first time ever I realized how screwed up my values were in life. Here I was, 'proving something to the world', working 14-hour days to make more and more money, only to have almost lost my whole family.

That day was a defining moment in my life as it led to the darkest soul-searching journey. We lost 126 neighbors that summer – 126! It was beyond devastating! And, while we were in the midst of mourning and helping rebuild, my financial business partner decided to take advantage of the situation and hijacked my business I had worked so hard to build. I went from being a multimillionaire to being left with a dollar coin on a table. Literally!

The disbelief, hurt and betrayal were beyond what I could handle. The emotional shutdown was so severe that it threw me into a place I have never experienced before – a place of absolute numbness. It took a long, long time to recover from so much loss – the loss of so, so many neighbors and very nearly my family, the loss of my business and, to my surprise, eventually the loss of my own personal identity.

What eventually got me out of that dark place was the positive outlook I had developed while doing personal development courses years earlier. See, someone once told me that life teaches you by giving you gifts wrapped in a problem – and the bigger the problem the bigger the gift inside.

I decided to take some time out and really re-evaluate my life and, most importantly, my **values** in life. I let go of the beautiful home, I let go of all the luxuries in life, I pulled my kids out of private school, which we could no longer afford, and we hit the road. What better way to find adventure out of that mess?

Equipped with my Nikon and a passion for photography, we spent the next two years living out of a caravan (travel trailer), travelling the world. We just drove with no particular destination in mind, first around Australia, and then 50,000 miles through every state of the USA. We immersed ourselves in different cultures, from Aboriginal tribes in Australia to Navajo Indians in Arizona, from Eskimos in Alaska to the Amish in Pennsylvania. We rode horses with cowboys in Texas, danced with the Salvos on the streets of New York, hiked 40 national parks and played music with buskers in Nashville.

The beauty about travelling with young children is that it shows you life through their innocent perspective. We were all born loving, caring, generous, playful, trusting, compassionate and non-judgmental. But somehow as we grow older life gets 'real' and we shut off certain parts of us in the name of 'safety'. Watching life through our kids' perspective brought it all back to light.

Dropping back to basics and regaining trust in humanity, we opened ourselves to experiences and saying yes to everything that came our way. I cannot tell you how much this has enriched our lives. The golden nuggets of wisdom we have found whilst sharing a sandwich with the homeless, by volunteering at animal rescue shelters, from meeting humans from all walks of life and by saying yes to different experiences are priceless!

Having had conversations with hundreds of people made me really realize how many of us are engulfed by what I now call the 'success trap': wasting our hours doing work we sometimes hate to afford stuff which doesn't fulfill us and trying to impress people we don't even like. We sacrifice our health to make money so that later in life we can spend the money trying to regain our health. We have families but we are not really present – often caught up in our heads about stuff we need to do. We are always busy chasing the mirage of happiness in some unforeseen future.

A week turns into a month, a month turns into a year, a year turns into a decade and before you know you it, in a blink of an eye, your life is gone and you stop and look back with regret and realize that you had only one shot at life and you let it slip by.

This travel opened my eyes to the mind trap most humans are in and how our limiting beliefs determine where we end up. We are all conditioned by our society as to what the definition of success should look like that we never stop to question ourselves 'why' – why are we the way we are; why do we do the stuff we do; what is it that we really want out of life?

With those questions in mind, I embarked on a serious journey of self-discovery. I have always had immense interest in human psychology and personal growth, and being an overachiever by nature I've tracked down and studied and learned from the best in the world. The same mind that once built a quarter-billion-dollar empire, with no money to start with, was once again put to work – this time to find best solutions for human fulfillment.

Hundreds of books and seminars later, I have learned how the mind truly works and how to re-code it at your own will. I used my business skills to redesign my whole life's blueprint, and my painful experiences and healing to redefine my values in life.

I've learned why on earth I am such an overachiever and why it was important to 'prove myself to the world'. When you discover the quirky programs that run your life, you will be dumbfounded to learn why you've turned out the way you have. But what's even more enlightening is that, by learning this, you can set yourself free.

Just like for a successful business, your life requires a plan, a blueprint that will encompass all your life's categories: your personal, your professional and your spiritual life.

The most important thing is finding your North Star: your true, authentic self. If you can find what your purpose in life is, what your heart truly desires, everything else will just fall into place. Your work will no longer be work but fulfillment. Your friendships, relationships and passion projects will not need to be balanced as everything will fit in like an amazing puzzle. Life will no longer be a never-ending hamster wheel – it will be a thrilling, satisfying and soulful adventure.

I now live the most fulfilling life! I have deep friendships, incredible family, and a satisfying career in business and life coaching; I travel to amazing places, do volunteer work with kids, learn from the best, have lots of creative passion projects and attract the most amazing humans into my life.

I no longer miss my anniversaries but am present for all of my family and friends. I cherish every moment with them and make our time together special.

I no longer go on holidays and miss what's there – I throw myself into experiences and get the true essence of every place I go to, and create lifelong friendships wherever I go.

I'm no longer the person whose life insurer tells them they're uninsurable – I value my health above all and plan to live to a rocking 100!

I no longer run my life to prove anybody wrong – I live to empower humans to live their true potential!

The process that you will discover in this book is years of knowledge and experience condensed into this skinny little book. Don't let the small volume fool you – I am a 'no bullshit', straight-to-the-point kinda girl, hence I have diluted the complexities of psychology and quantum physics, removed all the academic jargon, de-fluffed the unnecessary – and converted all this into a usable step-by-step process. This book will take you from stress, fogginess and lack of direction towards clarity, fulfilment and life beyond your wildest dreams!

Do yourself a favour and read it cover to cover. Don't wait for a tragedy to jumpstart you into living – work out what you want from life and live it now!

Enjoy your journey!

Anna

"This book is amazing! It is changing my life and it will do the same for you! It is a joy to read and simplifies what should surely be complex concepts! I am so grateful and can't wait to see what the future has in store for me!"

Susan Wieland, Fishburn, UK

"Anna's refreshing perspective gives a unique, insightful and fun approach to self-improvement. With the Quantum Mind Academy in support, I'm really looking forward to the journey ahead of me."

David Wharf, Bristol, UK

"Anna, it's amazing how the Universe provides at exactly the right time. Many years ago we were lucky enough to cross paths. You had a huge impact on my life then and have continued to enter my life throughout the years at exactly the right moment in time. Eternally grateful our lives intersected. I am going through a major life event at the moment. Out of the blue there you are with this life-changing book and journal to assist not only me but my family at the exact moment we need guidance and support. I am on a journey of growth and personal development. I have been searching for the right path to follow and the tools to aid my journey. You are an incredible role model and inspiration for all women and men alike. I can't wait to see you catching up with Oprah to chat about your book and program. Completing the circle. Love and light."

Vicky Chalmers, Melbourne, Australia

"If you want to create your life the way you want and feel empowered at the same time, this book is for you!"

Gayatri Kuraganti, Lexington, SC, USA

> "I Am –
> Two of the most powerful words;
> for what you put after them shapes
> your reality"
> Bevan Lee

www.ingramcontent.com/pod-product-compliance
Lightning Source LLC
Chambersburg PA
CBHW020947230426
43666CB00005B/203